Contemporary Mexican Drama in Translation

Volume II:

No One Knows Anything

by Vicente Leñero

Introduction and translations
by Myra S. Gann

Danzón Press
14 Hamilton St.
Potsdam, N.Y. 13676

© Myra S. Gann, 1995
ISBN 0-9643288-1-X

Library of Congress
Catalog Card Number
94-69405

CONTENTS

Introduction

Vicente Leñero   1
Stage Directions   5

Act One   7
Act Two   62

INTRODUCTION
(reprinted from Volume I)

"As strange as it may seem, the decade of the crisis has been the decade of the boom in Mexican dramaturgy" ["Por extraño que parezca, la década de la crisis ha sido la del auge de la dramaturgia mexicana"]. Thus began an article published in *Semanal*, the weekly cultural supplement of the daily *La Jornada*, in the last issue of the decade (José Ramón Enríquez, "La dramaturgia mexicana en su auge de crisis," #28, Dec. 24, 1989, pp. 20-25).

During the seventies it was commonly accepted that plays written by living Mexicans, unless Emilio Carballido were the author, would be seen only in very experimental theaters, produced by marginal groups who dared take a great risk, since theatergoers (supposedly) consistently preferred contemporary American and European, or classical anything, to national drama. But the eighties were different. During this decade Víctor Hugo Rascón Banda and Oscar Liera had at least one major production every year, while Jesús González Dávila and Vicente Leñero were staged seven times. And Tomás Urtusástegui, who before 1980 had never written a play, had his first professional performance in 1982 and saw a new play produced every year until 1989, when in different parts of the country, in amateur and professional contexts combined, there were over sixty different productions of his plays. The number of dramatic composition workshops multiplied, launching many new playwrights, including, for the first time, an increasing number of women. And, of course, Emilio Carballido continued to supply theater companies with outstanding works, approximately one every other year, his comedy *Rosa de dos aromas* setting the national record for the longest single run of any play. The general feeling among playwrights was that the tides had changed, that directors and producers were actually hungry for new Mexican plays, that they were being preferred over imports, and that there was an unprecedented interest in examining Mexican reality, however painful that examination might be.

How can this remarkable change in popularity of the playwrights and in attitude of the theatergoers be accounted for? Some believe that the economic crisis itself was responsible, as Rascón Banda foresaw as early as 1982:

> ... maybe, faced with the impossibility of producing refried versions of North American or English plays, we will begin to draw on our national raw material; maybe, faced with the difficulty of obtaining funds to import second-class movies and third-class television programs, we will turn to the native-born to write, direct, act and produce. It could be that, faced with the lack of economic resources for productions of one, two and three million pesos, to which some privileged persons have become accustomed, we will have to rely on ingenuity, talent and creativity to substitute for devalued pesos. It may very well be...
>
> [...pudiera suceder que, ante la imposibilidad de producir refritos teatrales de Norteamérica e Inglaterra, se acuda a la materia prima nacional; pudiera ocurrir que, ante la dificultad de conseguir divisas para importar cine de segunda y televisión de tercera, se recurra a los nativos para escribir, dirigir, actuar y producir. Pudiera ser que, ante la falta de recursos económicos para las producciones de uno, dos y tres millones de pesos, a que tan mal se acostumbraron algunos privilegiados, se tenga que acudir al ingenio, al talento y a la creatividad, para suplir la carencia de los devaluados pesos. Bien pudiera ser...] ("Nueva dramaturgia mexicana," *Latin American Theatre Review*, 18/2, spring 1985, p. 92.)

If Mexico was to have any theater at all during those years, Rascón believed, it was to be Mexican theater, the only affordable one. In addition, playwrights seeing opportunities opening up began to tailor their works to the crisis situation, making them even more appealing: a large percentage of the plays written during this period have a very small cast of characters and can be performed in black box theaters with few or no props. These dramatists often joke that they have found the true meaning of Jerzy Grotowski's "poor theater."

It must also be remarked that the efforts of Emilio Carballido, Hugo Argüelles and Vicente Leñero seemed to finally reach fruition in the eighties. These more established playwrights devoted a substantial amount of their time over the years, in Carballido's case ever since the late sixties, to the formation of the current generation of playwrights, the "New Dramatists" and the "New New Dramatists" as well. It is to Carballido's decade-long writing workshop held at the Polytechnic Institute and his subsequent constant mentoring of young writers, along with Arguelles' and Leñero's workshops of the late seventies and entire eighties, that most of the plays which reached the stage during the "boom" of the eighties can be attributed.

The four playwrights selected for this volume were active participants in the Leñero workshop, Vicente Leñero always insisting that he was not a "teacher" but, rather, an organizing force behind the workshop, a participant in the same way as the others. The plays themselves, Leñero's in particular, reflect the interest of this group in returning the dramatic text to its rightful place in the theater--first place-- and, similarly, in experimenting with new realisms, with the intention of expressing more faithfully the disjointed, non-teleological view of reality of the eighties.

After years of seeing the text used as a "pretext" for the theatrical event, the Leñero playwrights called for a renewed respect for the written word and for authors to have a place at least equal to that of the director in the making of the final product (see Azcárate et al, "Textos y pretextos del teatro mexicano: once dramaturgos debaten sobre los textos, los pretextos, los montajes y las rutas del teatro mexicano," in *Semanal*, #24, Nov. 26, 1989, pp. 26-33). They saw themselves as distinct from playwrights of previous "text-centered" movements who considered themselves "men of letters" rather than "men of the theater" and for whom publication of the play was as satisfactory as a production of it. These dramatists of the eighties were writing with the stage and its audience in mind at all times, production being their primary goal, even though they chose to give priority to the word (and what it *does*) over actions (and what they *say*) (see Leñero's article "Dramaturgia para hoy o para nunca" in *Proceso* 755, April 22, 1991, pp. 48-49).

The return to realism was a direct result of the renewed emphasis on the text, and led to Rascón's poetic realism, Leñero's hyperrealism, Azcárate's comic realism and Urtusástegui's combination of farce with realistic comedy. The realities depicted in these plays are very specifically Mexican, without falling into the *costumbrismo* of previous generations, which frequently created light-hearted descriptions of local color, mostly rural. The situations are fictitious, but the language and the motivations of the characters are extremely true to life; in the case of Leñero's *No One Knows Anything*, one of the characters was so recognizable as a Mexican dignitary that the play was closed down until the author made a few minor changes to make his character less reminiscent of the real-life model.

The four plays are quite representative of the overall national production of the eighties, especially with regard to theme; in them, as in a large number of works not included here, hypocrisy--with the corruption, deception and double standards that stem from it--is seen as the underlying cause of most of the problems facing Mexico today.

We can only conclude that Mexican drama of the eighties reflects the profound desire for change that can be felt in most areas of Mexican society today. But fortunately for us, these plays follow the classical Spanish norm of combining *enseñanza* ("teaching") with *deleite* ("pleasure"); they are as pleasurable to read as they are informative about contemporary Mexican society.

Groups or individuals interested in obtaining permission to perform the plays can make contact with the playwrights through me.

--Myra S. Gann
--State University of New York at Potsdam

Vicente Leñero, born in Guadalajara in 1933, was a relative latecomer to the theater and to writing, his first career having been that of engineer. Currently one of the most renowned figures among Mexico's intelligentsia, he has written nine novels, fifteen plays, two collections of short stories and several works of non-fiction; and since 1976 he has been managing editor of the prestigious *Proceso*, a journal of political analysis and criticism. Very central for contemporary Mexican dramaturgy was the dramatic composition workshop he held weekly in his house for over ten years (1975-1991), discussed in the general introduction to these two volumes.

From the opening of his very first play, *Pueblo rechazado*, in 1968, Leñero has been controversial: he is always at the same time profoundly Catholic yet extremely irreverent, a member of the establishment while vehemently critical of it; in many of his plays he questions or subverts the official versions of events in Mexican history. In *Vivir del teatro* (1982), his autobiography of his years in the theater, he details the arduous process of getting each of his plays approved by the "performance authorities" ("autoridades de espectáculos"); *No One Knows Anything (Nadie sabe nada)*, which opened six years later, directed by Luis de Tavira, encountered the same difficulties and caused a ruckus loud enough to be heard by the *New York Times* ("A New Play Dissects Mexico's Press, and It's Not a Pretty Sight," Aug. 28, 1988, NR H 33). After running only eight days its own sponsor (the Instituto Nacional de Bellas Artes) abruptly closed it, citing "orders from above" (see *La Jornada*, May 27, 1988, 17). Public pressure forced the Institute to reopen it, however, and it ran several months beyond its originally projected season.

Leñero's dramatic composition workshop introduced on to the Mexican stage the style known as "hyperrealism," a "real realism," according to Leñero, which is related to yet goes beyond the naturalism of the earlier part of our century. A natural extension of the documentary theater for which Leñero was already known, this realism tries to be photographic in nature, to do away with the traditional artifices which are used to create the illusion of the fourth wall, to match the time of the spectator with the time of the characters in the play more closely than in traditional realism. It does not feel compelled to provide complete background information for a plot or a character, to explain the cause behind every effect, or even to tie up all loose ends by the end of the play.

As we read in the opening stage directions, *No One Knows Anything* is one of these plays. Thus, every scene bears an exact indication of the time of day it occurred; and we are presented with numerous seemingly extraneous details, such as the type of flowers considered by a customer at the Flower Stand, and the ones she finally chooses. Similarly, we will read in the stage directions at one point that "possible agents" have ransacked an apartment: here, if the spectator does not know who the perpetrators were, if the characters don't either, then neither does the writer of the stage directions, who is traditionally much more omniscient than this. Finally, the fact that the contents of the documents which are at the heart of this "thriller" are never revealed to the reader/spectator, even though the protagonist does get a chance to read them, will frustrate the reader or spectator who has no experience with hyperrealism, where lack of closure is common.

As staged by Luis de Tavira, this play was apparently difficult to follow, packed as it was with theatrical devices and hyperrealistic details such as a real Volkswagen crossing the stage when Pepe and Juan Jose are shot at in the Taco Restaurant. The elaborate simultaneous sets made for an extremely interesting spectacle, but were distracting for the spectator trying to follow the complicated "whodunnit" type plot. But it is a real "page-turner" for readers and possesses a potential for being staged not realized by Tavira. It made an important mark on the history of Mexican theater and is well worth being brought to the attention of readers outside of Mexico.

NO ONE KNOWS ANYTHING

by Vicente Leñero

The action occurs in Mexico City, now, over a three-day period of one week (Monday, Tuesday and Wednesday) (Act One), and three days of the following week (Monday, Tuesday, Wednesday) (Act Two).

Scenic spaces:

1- News room
2- Apartment building on Serapio Rendón. Stairwell; interior and exterior of Apartment 5, and interior and exterior of a neighboring apartment.
3- Cantina. Open room and rest rooms.
4- Street. Public area, telephone with plastic shell-type booth (not closed), flower stand, newspaper stand, alley, etc.
5- Casablanca Club. Collective steam bath; massage and dressing area, with a series of lockers.
6- Government Offices. Two connecting offices.
7- Taco Restaurant
8- Gerda's House. A small living room.
9- Cabaret. Dance floor and area with tables.

Notes on scenic spaces:

1- The scenic spaces are intended to be hyperrealistic.
2- The spaces should be simultaneously present from the beginning to the end of the play.
3- During each scene, each one of these spaces will have a life of its own for the duration of the scene. The main action will control the narration, but should in no way prevent what is happening in the other spaces from being understood.

ACT ONE

SCENE 1

Week 1. Monday morning. Between 10 and 11 a.m.

Main action: Space 1: News room

> **Simultaneous actions:**
>
> **Space 2: Apartment Building**
>
> *Dalila is sleeping, nude, in her apartment (apartment number 5). In the neighboring apartment: Neighbor is washing dishes in the sink. Later she leaves and notices that the light on the stairwell is out. She gets angry. She returns to her place and takes a bulb from one of her lamps. Carrying the bulb and a chair, she goes out to the landing. She tries to screw the bulb into the socket, but for a long time can't manage it. She keeps trying.*
>
> **Space 4: The Street. Different angles.**
>
> *Gerda crosses the street pulling a little market basket. Under her arm she is carrying a picture wrapped in manila paper. She greets the passersby. She gives a tangerine to a shoeshine boy who is shining Agent 2's shoes. When she reaches the flower stand, she chats at length with the Florist about plants currently in season. She would like to buy marigolds, but there aren't any, the Florist tells her. She finally buys some gladiolas and disappears.*
>
> *While Agent 2 is having his shoes shined by the Shoeshine Boy, Agent 1 guards the building where the newspaper's offices are located. He is watching the people going in and out, and the window from which, perhaps, Salcido can be seen. Efren appears in the street, whistling. He speaks briefly with Agent 2.*

Space 5: The Casablanca Club

Pato the Masseur is giving a client a massage. Inside the steam room, the reporter Toño Tena is recovering from a hangover. He is naked, under the steam, drinking a beer. Later he takes a shower, shaves and starts to dress.

Space 6: Government Offices

In her office, High Official talks on the phone. The red network telephone rings and she suspends her call to pick up the red phone and answer it, standing up. One senses in her an attitude of extreme obedience. She hangs up and sits down again.

Also in his office, Low Official speaks with Moctezuma Peon. The latter then very cautiously hands the former what we surmise to be an envelope of cocaine. Low Official later takes Moctezuma Peon into the office of High Official.

Outside the government building, Moctezuma's Assistant reads a Superman comic book while he waits for his boss.

Space 7: Taco Restaurant

The Taco Restaurant, like the Cantina and the Cabaret, is closed. We know this because the metal curtain is down. The Taco Seller arrives at his establishment on a bicycle after having gone to sell gelatin desserts (his second job) prepared by the Neighbor. When he tries to open the curtain, the Taco Seller realizes he has forgotten the key to the padlock. He gets on his bicycle and goes to look for it.

Space 1: News room

The news room of the paper, almost empty. Only one of the reporters' desks is occupied: that of Juan Jose Tagle (a journalist in his thirties), who is typing, occasionally consulting a stenographer's notebook.

In the receptionist's area is Rosamaria Patiño (twentiesh), in front of a desk covered with telephones which she is in charge of answering. She is also typing: she is transcribing a Dictaphone tape which she is listening to through earphones.

Very close to Rosamaria, in one of the armchairs in the improvised receptionist's area, Lorenzo Salcido waits. He is fortiesh; he wears a suit; he checks his wristwatch frequently.

One of the telephones rings. Rosamaria stops typing, disconnects the Dictaphone and picks up the receiver.

ROSAMARIA: *(Into the phone)*
--News room...
–
--No, he's not in. He's sure to be back by seven. May I help you?
–
--Certainly.
–
--Certainly.
–
--Yes, of course. I'll tell him.

Rosamaria hangs up and writes in a notebook. She continues her transcription. Visibly impatient, Salcido interrupts Rosamaria.

SALCIDO: The reporters don't come in 'til afternoon, right?
ROSAMARIA: *(Taking off her earphones to attend to Salcido)* I beg your pardon?
SALCIDO: Sorry. *(Changing tone.)* The reporters--they won't be in until late afternoon?
ROSAMARIA: Six-thirty. But Pepe will be right back.
SALCIDO: Are you sure?
ROSAMARIA: *(Pointing to her machine)* He has to pick up this transcription.

Rosamaria continues her task. Juan Jose stops typing. He gets up and goes to a small table near Rosamaria's desk. While he pours himself some coffee from the electric coffeepot, he speaks to Salcido.

JUAN JOSE: If you want me to give Pepe a message, or tell him something, I'm perfectly willing, Mr. Salcido... Do you remember me?
SALCIDO: Of course.

JUAN JOSE: Pepe and I work together on important stories. Remember last time? I was working with him.
SALCIDO: Oh, yeah...
JUAN JOSE: It's up to you.
SALCIDO: I'd like to speak with him personally. *(He stands. He shows signs of leaving.)* I'll come back later.
JUAN JOSE: You're not leaving?
SALCIDO: I'm a little pressed for time. I'll come back later.
JUAN JOSE: Would you like Pepe to call you at a certain number?
SALCIDO: I'll call him later.
JUAN JOSE: It's up to you.
ROSAMARIA: *(Stops typing)* You really should wait for him. He won't even be a minute.
SALCIDO: I'll call him later. Thank you. *(He waves good-bye to Juan Jose. He forces a smile.)* If you'll excuse me.

Salcido leaves the office. Juan Jose follows him with his eyes, until he disappears from sight.

Space 4: The Street

When Agent 1, who is guarding the newspaper building, sees Salcido leave, he whistles insistently toward Agent 2. In response to the signal, Agent 2 interrupts his shoeshine and his conversation with Efren and goes to meet Agent 1; the two of them leave, in pursuit of Salcido.

Salcido has not seen his pursuers, but he senses that they are following him. He leaves the set, as do Agents 1 and 2.

ROSAMARIA: Who is he?
JUAN JOSE: Pepe's Throat.
ROSAMARIA: Who?
JUAN JOSE: Pepe's Deep Throat. Sometimes he gives Pepe tips, like in the movies... If this were a real newspaper, we'd stir up big trouble with the stuff he gets us.
ROSAMARIA: Like what kind of stuff?
JUAN JOSE: Information. Documents. Remember that series on telephone espionage? *(Changes tone.)* That's right, you weren't here yet. That was two years ago.
ROSAMARIA: What happened?

JUAN JOSE: A story Pepe and I wrote, with transcriptions we got from Salcido. Too bad Sagrario didn't have the guts to publish more than about half, but even so...
ROSAMARIA: Oh, yeah, Pepe told me about that.
JUAN JOSE: And the lists of the big shots who converted all their money into dollars and sent it out of the country.
ROSAMARIA: He got those too?
JUAN JOSE: Yeah, but no one knows that. Shhh. Not even Sagrario. It's a secret. Just between Pepe and Salcido. Very confidential.

Rosamaria resumes her work. Instead of returning to his place, Juan Jose begins to caress Rosamaria, rubbing her shoulders.

ROSAMARIA: What are you doing? Cut it out. Pepe will be here any minute.
JUAN JOSE: Big deal.

The Errand Boy of the news room enters. He's very young.

ERRAND BOY: *(Who has taken in the scene, to Juan Jose)* Your cigarettes, man.
JUAN JOSE: What about Rosamaria's?
ERRAND BOY: Just be glad I got you yours. Marlboros have gone up.
JUAN JOSE: I gave you enough for two packs.
ERRAND BOY: Like I said, the Marlboros cost more now.
JUAN JOSE: Don't try to fool me, boy.
ERRAND BOY: I don't have to do anything for that cat.
ROSAMARIA: This "cat" wants no favors from anyone, much less from you, you pip-squeak.
JUAN JOSE: You go get me those cigarettes or you'll be real sorry.
ERRAND BOY: Didn't you hear? She doesn't want 'em anymore.
JUAN JOSE: You'd better remember this when I give you "what for," you stinking kid.
ERRAND BOY: OK, OK...

The Errand Boy leaves. Juan Jose and Rosamaria take up their erotic game again.

ROSAMARIA: *(While Juan Jose caresses her)* And where does he get his information from?

JUAN JOSE: Salcido? I don't know. Who knows.

They kiss.

JUAN JOSE: Are you really getting married?
ROSAMARIA: In March.
JUAN JOSE: Really, Rosamaria?
ROSAMARIA: Stop that, now.
JUAN JOSE: Ah, I'm in heaven.
ROSAMARIA: Get away.
JUAN JOSE: So you're serious?
ROSAMARIA: About what?
JUAN JOSE: Getting married.
ROSAMARIA: Of course I'm serious.
JUAN JOSE: You don't love him.
ROSAMARIA: I love him very much.
JUAN JOSE: What about me?
ROSAMARIA: Come on, Juancho, don't start this again. (*Pushes him away.*) Leave me alone.

A telephone rings. Rosamaria breaks away from Juan Jose to answer it, but he keeps on with his caresses. While Rosamaria talks and listens, Juan Jose puts his hand down the front of her blouse and fondles her breasts.

ROSAMARIA: *(Into the phone)*
--Good afternoon. News room.
--
--No, he's not here. He won't be in until seven.
--
--*(Distracted by Juan Jose's caresses, she tries to get free from him.)* I'm sorry. What was that?. . . What?
--
--Certainly.

Rosamaria writes on a piece of paper and waves her hand to free herself from Juan Jose. She achieves this almost at the same time Pepe (thirtiesh) enters the news room. We don't know if Pepe has noticed the erotic advances of Juan Jose toward Rosamaria. She continues talking on the phone while Pepe looks in his mailbox and reads a few papers he takes from it. Juan Jose returns to his place and resumes typing.

No One Knows Anything

ROSAMARIA: *(Into the phone)*
--I'll give him your message. I wrote it down right here.
–
--Certainly.
–
--Glad to be of help.

Rosamaria returns quickly to her transcription while Pepe continues to read the papers he found in his box.

ROSAMARIA: *(To Pepe)* I'm more than half way through. It'll be done in half an hour.

Pepe crosses to his desk, caressing Rosamaria's chin gently as he passes her. Rosamaria gives him some pages as he passes.

ROSAMARIA: The first tape turned into fifteen pages. That's the most important part, isn't it?
PEPE: The end of the tape you've got is real important, too. That's where the lead is.
ROSAMARIA: I'll be done in a half hour. Forty-five minutes at the most.

Juan Jose works at his desk, as does Pepe.

Space 2: Apartment Building

Salcido, followed at some distance by Agents 1 and 2, enters the building, right at the moment when the Neighbor, who has climbed on to a chair, is trying to screw a light bulb into the fixture on the stairwell. Salcido trips. The Neighbor is about to fall, but Salcido helps her. She rejects him energetically:

NEIGHBOR: *(To Salcido)* Get away from me! Don't come near me!

At that moment, the Neighbor sees Agents 1 and 2, who have appeared after Salcido.

NEIGHBOR: *(To the Agents)* What are you looking at? Go stare at the freaks in the circus!

The agents flee the building and disappear from stage.

NEIGHBOR: *(To Salcido)* See what you cause by stealing the light bulbs? You almost made me kill myself! But don't worry about me, after all, light bulbs grow on trees, don't they?

Salcido goes into Apartment 5 and closes the door in the Neighbor's face. He looks at Dalila, asleep in the room, and he caresses her briefly. Later he busies himself going through some papers, consulting notebooks, looking in drawers.

The Neighbor finishes putting in the light bulb and returns to the interior of her apartment, where she continues her activities.

JUAN JOSE: *(To Pepe)* Calvo wants your interview before six because he's gonna put it on the first page. He told me to tell you.

The Errand Boy returns. He throws the cigarettes at Juan Jose, but Juan Jose returns them to him and points to Rosamaria.

ERRAND BOY: *(To Juan Jose)* You give 'em to her, for Christ's sake. *(He stops short when he sees Pepe. He changes attitude. Falsely:)* Here're the Marlboros you asked me for, Rosita. They were out of "lights"; I brought you the red pack, like Juan Jose's. *(He goes toward Pepe.)* Good afternoon, sir. Guess what? We lost.
PEPE: What's that?
ERRAND BOY: We lost.
PEPE: Lost what?
ERRAND BOY: The numbers, sir. I told you. You see what happens when you won't even place one double? We only got nine. *(Changing tone.)* You know what's wrong? Like Tomas said the other day: There's no originality in this country anymore. That's what's wrong.
JUAN JOSE: *(Interrupting him)* Don't be ridiculous, boy. Just shut up. Get out of here. Out! Get to work!
ERRAND BOY: Hey, man, what's the matter? What's eatin' you?

The Errand Boy leaves. Juan Jose and Pepe take up their conversation again.

JUAN JOSE: *(To Pepe)* See what you think of this opening. *(Reading, without taking the page out of the typewriter.)* "Several groups from the business sector and the clergy are attempting to challenge Mexico's power structure; however, they have forgotten that the worker's movement is an obstacle to their political aspirations," said Fidel Velazquez Sanchez, General Secretary of the etcetera, etcetera. What do you think?

Pepe nods his head slightly.

JUAN JOSE: I have another statement. Let's see. *(Reading from a notebook:)* "The next increase in the minimum wage will not totally restore the loss of purchasing power of the middle class. . . bla bla bla, but. . . but we will do everything possible to obtain an amount which will alleviate to some degree the situation of the workers." *(Changing tone.)* The other one's better. Don't you think? I just have those two.
PEPE: It's better.
JUAN JOSE: The first one.

Pepe nods.

JUAN JOSE: His statements are all empty-sounding. Fidel's getting old. . . Not worth much anymore. *(Changing tone.)* Hey, by the way. Your Deep Throat came by to see you.
PEPE: Who?
JUAN JOSE: Salcido. He just left.
PEPE: Salcido?
JUAN JOSE: He just left. Not more than two minutes ago.
PEPE: What did he say?
JUAN JOSE: Nothing. Just that he'd call you later. He was acting very mysterious, as always.

Juan Jose takes up his typing again and Pepe goes back to looking through his papers. From the street, where he has been having his shoes shined, Efren Malvido enters. He is a reporter in his forties. He ad libs greetings to everyone, speaks to them adlibitum; maybe he pours himself some coffee. He then takes a seat at a desk where he will start typing. He will whistle from the moment he enters until the end of the scene.

Space 6: Government Offices

In the Office of Low Official, Low Official speaks with Assistants A and B.

In the Office of High Official, High Official exchanges a few words with Moctezuma Peon.

MOCTEZUMA PEON: I don't know anything about the content, but I was told to get them back this very week. That's why the boss is asking for some cooperation.
HIGH OFFICIAL: Do you need men?
MOCTEZUMA PEON: I just need you to let me decide how to handle it. Free rein.
HIGH OFFICIAL: You've got it, Moctezuma... And tell your boss he can count on us for whatever he needs.

Rosamaria stops transcribing for a moment and goes to Pepe.

ROSAMARIA: Coffee?

Pepe nods. Rosamaria pours coffee and takes it to Pepe. She speaks to him with a certain intimacy.

ROSAMARIA: How's it going?
PEPE: Fine.

The telephone rings. Rosamaria hurries to answer it.

Simultaneous sets:

Rosamaria is talking to Salcido, who is in Apartment #5, Space 2 (Apartment Building). Salcido is in front of a secretaire, barely illuminated by a lamp. He speaks in a low voice, cupping his hand around the voice piece. Dalila is still lying on the sofa.

ROSAMARIA: *(Into the phone)* Good morning. News room.
SALCIDO: *(Into the phone)* I'd like to speak with Gutierrez... Mr. Jose Gutierrez.
ROSAMARIA: Who's calling, please?

SALCIDO: Wolfgang Reintenbach.
ROSAMARIA: Who?
SALCIDO: Reintenbach Haussman.
ROSAMARIA: Who? *(Pause. She covers the telephone and goes to Pepe.)* It's for you.

Pepe gets up and takes the phone.

PEPE: *(To Rosamaria)* Who is it?
ROSAMARIA: I couldn't understand him. Some strange name.
PEPE: *(Into the phone)* Gutierrez speaking.
SALCIDO: *(Into the phone)* This is Salcido. I was just at your office.
PEPE: Oh, yeah, how are you?
SALCIDO: I can't explain the details on the phone. I'd like to see you right now.
PEPE: Right now?
SALCIDO: I've got some papers I know you'll be interested in, friend. Fresh documents... Just two days ago they were still on the President's desk.
PEPE: Really?
SALCIDO: Can you get here quick?
PEPE: Where?
SALCIDO: I'll give you the address. I'm on Serapio Rendon.
PEPE: *(Interrupting)* Let me write this down. *(He looks for a piece of paper, gets ready to write.)* OK.
SALCIDO: 24 Serapio Rendon. Apartment 5. Please come as soon as you can.

Suddenly Salcido is frightened. He hears noises in the building. In effect, Agents 1 and 2, his pursuers, can now be seen on the roof of the building.

SALCIDO: *(Nervous, into the phone)* See you later, Mr. Gutierrez. *(He hangs up the phone.)*

PEPE: Sure, I'll see you later. *(He hangs up.)*

After hanging up, Salcido begins to show signs of extreme nervousness. He leans out of a window into the stairwell and thinks he sees one of the Agents going onto or coming off of the roof. He puts

> on his jacket quickly. In quick succession he takes his portfolio, says a few words to Dalila and leaves the apartment and the building.

After hanging up, Pepe remains thoughtful for a few moments. Then he goes to his desk and from a drawer takes a slim portfolio.

PEPE: *(To Juan Jose)* That was Salcido.
JUAN JOSE: So soon? He just left.
ROSAMARIA: He used some strange name with me.
JUAN JOSE: Something big?
PEPE: Papers.
JUAN JOSE: What kind?
PEPE: He didn't say. He just told me where he got them.
JUAN JOSE: Where?
PEPE: From the President's desk.
JUAN JOSE: What president?
PEPE: The President of this country, who else?
JUAN JOSE: No shit!

With his portfolio in hand, Pepe crosses in front of Rosamaria as he heads toward the door to the street.

ROSAMARIA: You're leaving?. . Not even a kiss?

Pepe turns around slightly and blows her a kiss. Juan Jose gets up from his desk and goes to Rosamaria, not taking his eyes from where Pepe has just exited. The latter returns after having disappeared.

PEPE: Does Serapio Rendon run parallel to Miguel Schultz?
JUAN JOSE: Yeah, and to Sadi Carnot. It goes from San Cosme to Sullivan.

Pepe gestures his thanks and leaves again, rapidly. Juan Jose seems to remember something and takes a few steps to follow Pepe.

JUAN JOSE: What should I tell Calvo about your interview. . .

Pepe doesn't respond because he has already left. Juan Jose returns to where Rosamaria is. He speaks with a certain confidential air because of the presence--though distant--of Efren, who continues to whistle and type.

JUAN JOSE: I still don't understand why you want to marry that jerk... I guess he's good in bed.

Rosamaria smiles.

JUAN JOSE: Better than me?
ROSAMARIA: Different.

SCENE 2

Week 1. Monday morning. Between 11 and 12 a.m.

Main action: Space 2: Apartment Building

Simultaneous actions:

Space 1: News room

Rosamaria continues the transcription of Pepe's tape, while Juan Jose and Efren type at their respective desks. The Errand Boy cuts out articles from newspapers.

Space 4: The Street

The reporter "Ric" Ricardo Garcia walks up to a flower stand and orders a bouquet which the Florist prepares with special care. Ric pays for the bouquet, takes it and disappears. Later the Florist will arrange her stand and begin to eat the lunch she has brought in a pail.

Space 5: The Casablanca Club

There are no clients in the club. Pato the Masseur is cleaning the place: he scrubs the floors, washes the glass doors of the steam room. In the area of the lockers, the Shoeshine boy is polishing an enormous pile of shoes.

Space 6: Government Offices

Throughout the scene High Official sits in her office and signs document after document, assisted by Assistant A. In Low Official's office, Low Official is having a serious talk with Moctezuma Peon. When Low Official goes out for a moment, called by High Official, Moctezuma Peon quickly snorts some cocaine. At the end of the scene, Moctezuma Peon's Assistant comes to get his boss. He runs into Assistant B and trades his Superman comic book for the Novel of the Week. They also compare pistols. Moctezuma Peon and Moctezuma Peon's Assistant leave the area.

Space 7: Taco Restaurant

The Taco Seller reappears on his bike, carrying tools to open the metal curtain. During most of the scene he is trying to force the padlock open. At one point one gets the impression that he is not the owner of the Taco Restaurant, but, rather, a thief.

Space 8: Gerda's House

Gerda enters her house and starts to carry out an intimate celebration (it is the anniversary of her marriage to her dead husband). She unwraps the picture she was pulling in her market cart. It is a framed photograph of her and her husband with their two children: Chano Salcido and Dalila, still very young. Gerda hangs the picture, puts a Viennese waltz on the record player and opens a bottle of white wine from which she will drink a few glasses. Finally she falls on an armchair, pensive, tired, maybe a little sad.

Space 2: Apartment Building

Pepe approaches the Apartment Building. From the roof of the building, Agent 1 sees him and signals to Agent 2. The latter is making a call from a public telephone.

Simultaneous sets

Space 1: *In the news room the telephone rings. Rosamaria answers it. Agent 2 is calling from the public telephone booth.*

ROSAMARIA: *(Into the phone)* Good morning. News room.
AGENT 2: *(Into the phone)* Give me Efren Malvido.

> **ROSAMARIA:** *(She attracts Efren's attention)* Telephone, Efren.
>
> *Efren gets up from his desk and goes to Rosamaria's desk to take the call. The moment Efren takes the phone is exactly when Agent 1, from the roof of the Apartment Building, is signaling Agent 2 that Pepe is approaching. Agent 2 runs toward the place where Pepe is going to cross and leaves the receiver hanging.*
>
> **EFREN:** *(Into the phone)* Hello... hello! *(Irritated because no one answers, he hangs up.)*

Efren goes back to writing at his desk. From there he will observe how for the duration of most of the scene Juan Jose goes to Rosamaria and how they engage in very "private" discussions.

With his portfolio in hand, Pepe climbs the stairs of the old, dark, very deteriorated building. There are no numbers on the doors which open on to the stairwell. Pepe appears to be disoriented, trying to locate the right door. Coming down the stairs in the opposite direction is the Neighbor. She has just come out of her apartment. When Pepe approaches her, Agent 2, who at Agent 1's signal ran toward Pepe maybe to intercept him, has to give up his plan, preferring to slip away so that Pepe and the Neighbor will not catch on to his intentions.

PEPE: *(To the Neighbor)* Excuse me. Apartment five?

The Neighbor stops. She looks at him.

PEPE: Number five. Is it over there?
NEIGHBOR: Who are you looking for?
PEPE: I'm looking for Apartment five.
NEIGHBOR: No one's lived in number five for a long time. It's all closed up.
PEPE: *(After a silence, pointing to a door)* Is that it?

The Neighbor gives Pepe a last look and leaves the building. She goes to the public telephone booth, where she will remain until the end of the scene, refusing to budge even at the insistence of passersby.

Pepe hesitates in front of the door he pointed to minutes earlier. He knocks a couple of times. The he pushes the door with the palm of his hand. *At first the door doesn't move, but when he pushes a second time it moves slightly inward, with some difficulty, as if the wood were swollen. Pepe pushes until it is completely open. He hesitates to advance any further. The interior is completely dark.*

PEPE: Hello!

No one answers. Pepe finally gets up the nerve to take a few steps inside, into the darkness. He stumbles into something that seems like a hassock. Suddenly the room is filled with light. Someone has suddenly opened the Venetian blinds and the midday sun outlines the figure of a woman standing with the light behind her. She is Dalila: a woman of indefinite years who dresses like a spinster in mourning. Her mysterious air, her extravagance, don't impair her strange beauty. Pepe gradually recovers from the initial impact, but he is undoubtedly frightened.

PEPE: I'm sorry... The door... Is this number five? Apartment five?

Dalila nods.

PEPE: Mr. Salcido...

Dalila gestures to Pepe to enter. He does so as she closes the door and turns on the light of a small lamp that somewhat alleviates the darkness of the room filled with old furniture. We can make out a small table with two chairs, a secretaire and a large, overstuffed armchair.

PEPE: I'm looking for a Mr. Salcido... My name is Gutierrez.
DALILA: *(Looking at him while she recites, slowly, solemnly)*

> My heart lies when it says it loves you,
> turned into the faithful interpreter of my feeling,
> like the echo perceived in the abyss
> that the wind, not a voice, forms and spills.
>
> This imperious desire which reproaches you
> was not nurtured in the center of the soul:

it has disturbed me, without me, and like sound,
is foreign to my being, like a flame.

When blood saturates the heart
with your taste alone--middle term
of the crazy syllogism of bitterness--,

inaccessible to the implacable siege,
like a piece of lead in dark water
the soul sinks into delicious tedium.

Dalila has come quite close to where Pepe is standing, disconcerted.

DALILA: Do you like it?

Pepe doesn't respond.

DALILA: The poem.
PEPE: Yes... No... I don't know. I don't know anything about poetry.
DALILA: You're a writer.
PEPE: No, no, not a writer exactly. I'm a journalist. A reporter.
DALILA: You write.
PEPE: Well, sure. I write news pieces, articles, but...
DALILA: Have a seat, please. Would you like some herbal tea?
PEPE: No, thank you.
DALILA: Just a little cup. I've just prepared it, it's still hot. All I have to do is pour it. *(She goes toward an interior room.)* One sugar or two?

Dalila disappears into the interior room without waiting for a answer.

Space 3: Cantina

The Bartender noisily opens the metal curtain that covers the Cantina and immediately busies himself cleaning it. Toño arrives shortly. He is the night journalist of El Sol de Mexico, *an alcoholic and the lover of the waitress who works in the Cantina. He has a discussion with the bartender about old debts and ends up giving him his wristwatch as a guarantee of payment. The Bartender gives him a drink, which he drinks in solitude. Toward the end of the scene the waitress, Antonia, arrives. She doesn't have time to exchange words with her lover, Toño, because the Bartender scolds her for being late. He sends her off to clean the restrooms.*

While Dalila has been in the interior room, Pepe, disconcerted, examines the room he is in. He sits at a small table. Dalila returns with a steaming cup of tea, which she places in front of Pepe.

DALILA: I hope that's how you like it.

Observed carefully by Dalila, Pepe sips the tea.

DALILA: Too hot?
PEPE: No, it's fine. *(He takes another sip.)* Just fine.
DALILA: It's bougamvilia. Bougamvilia tea cures nostalgia, among other things.
PEPE: *(Sips the tea)* It tastes good.
DALILA: *(After a long silence)* Chano couldn't wait for you. He asked me to tell you.
PEPE: Salcido?
DALILA: He asked me to tell you.
PEPE: But he just called a few. . .
DALILA: *(Interrupting)* I said he couldn't wait. I never lie.

Silence.

PEPE: May I use your phone? To make a call?

Dalila nods. Pepe picks up the phone that is on the table where he is sitting; he dials.

Simultaneous scenes

Rosamaria's telephone rings in Space 1: News room. Pepe and Rosamaria converse over the phone.

ROSAMARIA: News room.
PEPE: Rosamaria. . . It's me.
ROSAMARIA: Pepe?
PEPE: Any messages? Has anyone called?
ROSAMARIA: No one.
PEPE: Salcido didn't call?

ROSAMARIA: No... Can I do anything for you?
PEPE: No, I'm on my way.

Pepe hangs up the phone. Rosamaria hangs up too.

Dalila stares at Pepe.

DALILA: I told you, I never lie. *(Pause.)* Chano will find you later. He told me to tell you.

Pepe gets up and starts to leave.

DALILA: Don't go please. Please don't go. You haven't finished your tea.

Pepe drinks his tea hurriedly, standing, and Dalila begins to recite another sonnet.

DALILA:

> To dream about the pale foliage
> and the plains where the wheat finishes,
> to aspire to solitude with you
> in the moist valleys and the forests;
>
> to seek the deep and savage region,
> to desire to possess you in secret,
> an embraced urge to be with you
> watching your face, an interior passageway:
>
> such was my most real youth;
> in the ideal climate of your sweetness
> my divine spring matured;
>
> and I had such a certain hope,
> that in fleeting beauty
> your beauty would be delivered unto me, intact.

Pepe begins to feel uncomfortable, because during her recitation Dalila seems to make erotic advances toward him.

DALILA: Nox. *(Pause.)* Nox. That's the name of the poem. Nox... by Concha Urquiza.
PEPE: Is your name Concha Urquiza?
DALILA: My name is Dalila... Concha Urquiza is the author of the sonnet. You've heard of her, haven't you?
PEPE: No.
DALILA: Really?
PEPE: No, I don't know anything about Concha Urquiza.
DALILA: No Mexican woman since Sor Juana has written such profound poetry. Erotic poems written for God, like those of Saint John of the Cross, like Saint Theresa's... *(She recites:)*

> Your warm presence separates me
> From the being who warms and the color that shines,
> closing off the senses in the vehemence
> of a night without depth and without border.

(Change in tone:) She drowned in the Pacific Ocean, near Ensenada, when she was 35, on the twentieth of June, 1945... She lived in pain, always searching for clarity. She went from Jesus to Marx. From the convent to the darkness of the Communist cell and back to the convent, to teaching, to the confessional . They say she was in love with a priest. They say she loved another woman. They say she took her own life. They say no: that the sea took her away because God was calling her... Concha Urquiza. Concepción Urquiza del Valle.

Pepe heads toward the door.

PEPE: That's interesting. She's an interesting woman. I'll read her stuff, everything I can find by her.
DALILA: Don't go.
PEPE: I'm leaving... Please tell Salcido that I was here and that... well, that I'm still willing to help if he wants. He'll understand. *(Pause.)* Thanks. Good-bye.

Pepe opens the door. In the stairwell are Agent 1 and Agent 2, who have been milling around the building during the whole scene.

DALILA: *(Emphatically)* Don't go yet, Pepe.

Pepe is shaken even more to hear his name. He forces a smile and leaves quickly. He closes the door as if in doing so he can prevent Dalila from catching up with him. Carrying his portfolio in his hand, he is about to descend the stairway when he sees Agents 1 and 2 blocking his way. He does not immediately realize that they are coming at him and when he does, it's too late. One of them punches him and the other tries to take the portfolio from him. Pepe is able to fend off the second one and tries to flee back up the stairs, but the men catch him. They beat him mercilessly; they kick him until he no longer moves and they leave him on the ground. Before running away, Agent 1 and Agent 2 frisk him: they take his wallet, his fountain pen, his watch; they kick him a few more times before they exit running down the stairs with his portfolio and belongings. They disappear into the street.

Space 7: Taco Restaurant

The Taco Seller is hammering away at the padlock which secures the metal curtain of his restaurant. It finally gives way and the curtain opens with a lot of clanging. The establishment is in plain sight. The Taco Seller begins his daily task of cleaning and straightening up.

DALILA: Oh, my God! *(Runs to him. Bends over him.)* What happened? What have they done to you?

Pepe moans. He can't speak.

DALILA: Who was it? *(She helps him straighten up.)* Here, let's see. Lean on me.

Helped by Dalila, Pepe manages to stand and, leaning on her, he moves toward the inside of her apartment. He is bleeding from the mouth, from the lip; he moans and pants continually.

DALILA: Don't worry, don't worry... it'll pass.

They enter the apartment. Dalila manages to steer him to the sofa, where he collapses.

DALILA: Do you feel really bad? Do you want me to call the police?
PEPE: No, no.

Dalila approaches him.

DALILA: Just look at what they've done to you.
PEPE: I'm better now. They knocked the wind out of me and...
DALILA: Don't push yourself. Some bougamvilia tea will make you feel better.

Dalila disappears into the interior room. Pepe tries to get up but doesn't have the strength. He tries to recover by breathing deeply.

Space 1: News room

The discussion between Juan Jose and Rosamaria has reached a climax. Rosamaria is clearly furious.

ROSAMARIA: How dare you, Juan Jose! You don't understand anything, do you? Don't you realize it's all over? No, you don't. You don't understand anything!

Rosamaria slaps Juan Jose.

JUAN JOSE: *(Controlling his anger)* No, I don't understand.

Efren gets up from his seat to try to mediate. He takes Juan Jose's arm and practically forces him to leave the News room. The two disappear. Rosamaria remains alone, at her desk, sniffling; she is watched from afar by the Errand Boy, who is still working on his task of cutting out articles.

Dalila returns to Pepe with a cup of tea. Pepe shakes his head negatively.

DALILA: Yes, you have to drink it. You'll feel better.

Pepe forces himself to drink the tea. He remains stretched out on the sofa, near Dalila, who is now sitting, watching him with tenderness.

DALILA: Poor thing, poor thing. *(Recites:)*

Your warm presence separates me
From the being who warms and the color that shines,
closing off the senses in the vehemence
of a night without depth and without border.

Dalila recites the last line with her mouth very near Pepe's face. They kiss. They embrace. Dalila's body falls over Pepe's, enveloping it.

SCENE 3

Week 1. Tuesday morning. Between 11 and 12 a.m.

Main action: Space 3: Cantina

Simultaneous actions:

Space 1: News room

There are no reporters in the News room. Rosamaria is typing and taking telephone messages. She occasionally tends to someone who comes up to ask her a question or leave correspondence for the reporters. The Errand Boy is arranging photos and making photocopies.

Space 2: Apartment Building

The Neighbor is preparing a meal in her apartment. She later goes up to the roof to hang out some laundry. Some intimate underwear is hanging on one of the lines on the roof. She is scandalized by a few of the articles and destroys them furtively, perhaps wrapping them in old newspaper and throwing the bundle down into the street, like garbage.

Space 4: The Street

High Official makes a brief round as she heads toward some destination for a possible inauguration. Along the curbs are groups of workers or peasants, certainly bused in for the occasion, waving little flags, carrying banners or cheering. High Official is accompanied by Low Official, by Sagrario (Managing Editor of the Newspaper) and by a few other officials. Assistants A and B are guarding the path of the group. Assistant A suddenly discovers the Shoeshine Boy and makes him give High Official a bouquet of flowers. The scene is photographed by one of the journalists who are with the group. The Shoeshine Boy is later given a tip for his services.

Space 6:   Government Offices

Offices of High Official and Low Official, empty. All of the workers appear to be at the ceremony. On High Official's desk, in an elegant vase, is the bouquet of flowers Ric Garcia gave to her in the previous scene.

Space 7:   Taco Restaurant

The Taco Seller is preparing the ingredients to make his tacos. He arranges soft drinks and beer in the refrigerator. He will later discover a rat and will try to kill it with a broom.

Space 8:   Gerda's House

Gerda converses with Salcido, her son. Agent 2 snoops around the outside of the house.

Space 3:   Cantina.   Interior room and restrooms

Liveliness and noise from the Cantina; it's happy hour. Four reporters are playing dominoes at one of the tables. Juan Jose Tagle and Toño Tena are playing against whistling Efren Malvido and "Ric" Ricardo Garcia. Except for Efren, they are all drinking beer. After each drink they place the bottles in corner bottle holders. Ric Garcia is eating a sandwich. During the game the players throw out, besides the looks they give each other, phrases and double entendres which are related to the particular play or to the person whose turn it is. Ric has just finished mixing the dominoes. They pick their pieces. They put them in order. Music from a juke box is heard. Noise. Smoke.

JUAN JOSE: *(To Toño)* You start.
TOÑO: Me?
JUAN JOSE: Come on.

EFREN: *(Joking, effeminate)* Come on, darling, I'm here.
TOÑO: OK, here goes. We'll start with the five. *(He places the double five in the middle.)* This one's gonna be your swan song... How much do we need?
JUAN JOSE: *(Consulting the score pad)* Twenty-two.
TOÑO: We need twenty-two.

Silence. They play.

> **Space 8: Gerda's House.**
> *Dalila enters. She gives her mother a quick kiss, as a greeting, and goes to Salcido.*
>
> DALILA: What's wrong? What did you call about?
> SALCIDO: Don't ask. Find Gutierrez at the newspaper and give him this *(He gives her a small envelope.)* Tell him... Listen to me: tell him I'll call him at ten tonight. Ten o'clock on the dot.
> DALILA: Where are you going to be?
> SALCIDO: I'll find you, don't worry.
> DALILA: Be careful.
>
> *Dalila gives Gerda another kiss and leaves the house, watched by Agent 2. When the scene is almost over we will see Dalila arrive at the News room of the newspaper, ask Rosamaria for Pepe (she doesn't know where he is), and receive from the Errand Boy the information that he might have gone to the Cantina.*
>
> *At Gerda's house, the old woman and Salcido are still talking.*

RIC: Tell us more, Efren. What happened? How much did he give you?
EFREN: Two hundred thousand.
RIC: Only two hundred thousand pesos? Sure!
TOÑO: But Sonora's a rich state.
RIC: Not if you compare it to Queretaro. Want to know how much the governor of Queretaro gave us when he gave his last state of the state address?
TOÑO: How much?
JUAN JOSE: *(Interrupting)* Play, guys. *(To Toño:)* I put down the blank. Pay attention.

EFREN: Cut the table talk.
TOÑO: I am paying attention. I've got the lead.

While the reporters play, Moctezuma Peon, at the bar, converses with the Bartender. Moctezuma Peon's Assistant is outside the Cantina, standing guard.

MOCTEZUMA PEON: *(Throws a martini glass to the floor)* This isn't a martini! This tastes like shit!
BARTENDER: Sir?
MOCTEZUMA PEON: Want me to show you how to prepare a real dry martini?
BARTENDER: You're on.
MOCTEZUMA PEON: First of all, the ice.

From this moment on, the Bartender follows all of Moctezuma Peon's instructions.

MOCTEZUMA PEON: Ice in the shaker... What temperature is your ice?
BARTENDER: It's cold.
MOCTEZUMA PEON: It should be kept close to zero, but, oh well. Ice. You put in the ice and you bathe it in a little vermouth... What kind of vermouth do you have?
BARTENDER: Cinzano.
MOCTEZUMA PEON: For a good martini, what you need is... let's say Noilly-Prat. Have you ever heard of Noilly-Prat?
BARTENDER: Never.
MOCTEZUMA PEON: Give me the Cinzano... A little squirt of Cinzano and a little squirt of coffee.
BARTENDER: Coffee?
MOCTEZUMA PEON: Coffee or coffee liqueur. But coffee's better. *(He pours a small amount of coffee out of a cup into the shaker.)* You shake it up good, you shake it up... And then you throw it all out.
BARTENDER: I throw it out?
MOCTEZUMA PEON: That's right. You throw it out. All you need is the aroma of the vermouth and the coffee that they've left on the ice... You throw it out and then, only then, do you put the gin in the shaker. Got any Old Pensioner?
BARTENDER: No.
MOCTEZUMA PEON: Beefeater?

BARTENDER: Just Oso Negro.
MOCTEZUMA PEON: Whatever. Oso Negro Gin. Oh well. You shake it up, shake it up. And there you have it. You serve it. Here, smell it! Perfect... And you crown your martini with an olive.

The game of dominoes is still going on at the table.

RIC: The gov of Queretaro gave five hundred big ones to all the reporters covering his speech.
EFREN: The same to everybody?
RIC: Well, those of us at the source got a little more, you know, to show the confidence they have in us. But the smallest wad was a full five-hundred. Plus the open bar and all the to-do. They even had chicks for those who wanted them, I swear to God.
JUAN JOSE: *(Putting down a domino)* Double one's.
RIC: *(Likewise)* Double three's.

During the domino game of dominoes, Pato the Masseur has entered the Cantina. Several times he tries to fondle Waitress Antonia. Toño notices this and reacts jealously:

TOÑO: *(To Waitress Antonia)* Hey, aren't you here to work?
ANTONIA: I *am* working.

Toño makes a move to get up from the table to slap her, but his friends stop him.

JUAN JOSE: *(To Toño)* Hey, bud, calm down.
EFREN: Take it easy.
RIC: *(To Antonia)* Pay him no mind, Antonia. Why suffer?
PATO THE MASSEUR: Cut it out, Toño, don't be ridiculous. What makes you think that I...
TOÑO: *(Persistent, to Antonia)* Working, yeah, working. *(He gets up and goes to the rest rooms.)* The first chance you get you do it with anybody.
WAITRESS ANTONIA: *(As if apologizing to all)* I haven't done anything. What is this?
RIC: Don't pay any attention to him. You know how he is.
JUAN JOSE: Ignore him, Antonia.
BARTENDER: Cut the talk, Antonia, get to work!

Waitress Antonia moves toward other tables.

BARTENDER: *(To the table of dominoes players)* Who's the don Pedro for?
RIC: Me.

Bartender takes him the drink. Toño returns from the rest room. Pato the Masseur approaches, conciliatory.

PATO: You're wrong, Toño. You need to leave her alone. She's got to earn a living.
TOÑO: Don't mess with me.
PATO: Whatever you say.
TOÑO: *(To Waitress Antonia, across the room)* See what you cause? Huh? Always!

Waitress Antonia flips him the "bird" with her middle finger. Toño did not see it. He goes back to his place. The game resumes.

TOÑO: Whose turn?
RIC: Yours.

They play.

EFREN: So. . . the gov gave you each half a melon.
RIC: That's when we get the most--the state-of-the-states.
EFREN: And on the tours.
RIC: When there are any.
TOÑO: For those of you at the source. Those of us who have to spread ourselves from one place to another are screwed. We don't get shit.
RIC: Weren't those workers gonna get you something? What happened there?
TOÑO: I'm still working on the watchman.
EFREN: I told you not to work for the *Sol de Mexico*. I told you. You bust your ass for nothing. No future there.
RIC: Well, the unions leave a pretty penny, don't they, Juan Jose? How much do they drop you every month? How much is in that envelope you get from the CTM?
JUAN JOSE: I don't get an envelope.
EFREN: Sure.
TOÑO: Really?

JUAN JOSE: No.
RIC: Sure you don't. Play dumb. You take whatever you can get. On the anniversary of the CTM, didn't you get a take? How much was it? A five-hundred spot?
JUAN JOSE: *(Smiling)* Well, only when they insist. Only when they insist a lot.
RIC: My ass.
EFREN: I let them give me my take too, because they can't corrupt me. If the money corrupted me, I wouldn't take it.

Laughter.

TOÑO: OK, that's enough, whose turn?
JUAN JOSE: Your play, Ric. I played the one's.
RIC: You think you're hot stuff, huh?
JUAN JOSE: Careful, I'm going out. Think about it.

Space 7: Taco Restaurant

The Taco Seller has finally managed to catch the rat. He kills it with a broom. Then he grabs the dead rat by the tail and throws it into the street, almost onto a crossing passerby who is holding a child's hand. The passerby screams wildly.

JUAN JOSE: Think about it.

Ric puts down a domino. Toño takes a turn. Efren takes a turn and Juan Jose puts his last piece down. Meanwhile, Pato the Masseur has left the Cantina, after talking secretly with Waitress Antonia: he has engaged her to work at an event at the Club next Monday evening.

JUAN JOSE: That's what I was looking for. I'm out.
EFREN: You're not paying attention, Ric. They're pissing all over us.
RIC: I thought you had the four.
EFREN: How could I have the four if my six got blocked when Toño put down his double?
JUAN JOSE: OK, OK, let's count. Do we have twenty-two there?
TOÑO: Make sure they count right.
EFREN: Nineteen.
TOÑO: Shit, three points. . . We only need three points. Ninety seven.

JUAN JOSE: We've got 'em this time.
TOÑO: *(Pointing)* Mixin' 'em up, boys, mixin' 'em up.

Efren mixes the pieces. Moctezuma Peon's Assistant, who has been on guard outside the Cantina, looks in and signals Moctezuma Peon. Almost immediately Pepe enters the Cantina. He goes toward the table of dominoes players. He has adhesive tape near his lower lip and a bruised cheek.

EFREN: Look who's here.
PEPE: *(Gestures a general greeting)* Hey.
TOÑO: You got beat up yesterday, Pepe? Juan Jose was just telling us about it.

Pepe nods.

EFREN: They leave you shitless?
PEPE: *(Leaning over to show his cheek)* See for yourselves.
TOÑO: Jesus, what a bitch.
RIC: *(Sarcastic)* Was it before or after you got the . . ?
PEPE: *(Smiling)* Before.
RIC: Well, that's something anyway. . .
EFREN: So, how much did they get?
PEPE: I didn't have much on me. Fifteen thousand pesos and my portfolio. And my wallet, with my i.d. and my license.
EFREN: That sucks.
PEPE: *(Changing tone, referring to the domino)* So who's winning?
JUAN JOSE: They're out after this round. We only need three points.

They select their pieces and stand them up, putting them in order.

PEPE: You playing every man?
EFREN: No, partners. But I've got to go, I'm late. You can have my place. . . See what you can do with Ric, poor ass hasn't seen a single play.
RIC: You're the ass; you only look out for your own skin. *(Change of tone:)* OK, let's go.

They play. Pepe, standing, watches over Juan Jose's shoulder. The latter talks to him somewhat confidentially.

No One Knows Anything 37

JUAN JOSE: No word from Salcido?
PEPE: Nothing.
JUAN JOSE: So why the beating?
PEPE: I don't think there was any connection. A simple mugging.
JUAN JOSE: Think so, huh?
PEPE: That's my guess.
JUAN JOSE: That rough?
PEPE: I've got to take a piss. When I get back, we'll stick it to 'em, Ric.
RIC: Sure thing.

Pepe crosses the room and goes toward the rest room. Moctezuma Peon and his Assistant, who has come in from the street, discreetly follow Pepe. Pepe goes into the rest rooms and prepares to urinate in front of a urinal. Moctezuma Peon and his Assistant wait for a customer to come out, so that the rest room is occupied only by Pepe; then they enter. The Assistant waits at the entrance, leaning on the door to obstruct passage. Pepe is slow to notice the spying presence of Moctezuma Peon. When he does, he looks alarmed.

MOCTEZUMA PEON: Easy, friend. Take your piss. Don't get scared.

Pepe hurries as much as he can. He finishes. He zips his pants.

MOCTEZUMA PEON: We understand you're a good friend of Lorenzo Salcido's. Is that correct?
PEPE: *(Stammering)* No, we're not friends. . .
MOCTEZUMA PEON: But you know him. You know him well enough to give him a message from me. My name is Moctezuma Peon, by the way.

Pepe acknowledges by nodding his head.

MOCTEZUMA PEON: *(Continuing)* And I'm real interested in purchasing some papers Salcido is selling. . . Unfortunately, I've been looking for him but can't find him and so I've had to come to you. *(Long pause. He watches Pepe's reactions carefully.)* Can you give him a message from me?
PEPE: I haven't seen him either. I haven't seen Salcido in a long time.

MOCTEZUMA PEON: *(Paying no attention to him)* Tell him, please, that I'm willing to pay him in dollars for the papers. Eighty thousand dollars the minute he hands them over. Cash *(Pause. He smiles.)* A respectable sum, wouldn't you say? And you could serve as the intermediary very nicely. *(Pause. From a pocket he takes out a calling card, which he gives to Pepe.)* Here's my phone number.

Pepe takes the card and looks at the number, automatically.

MOCTEZUMA PEON: I hope he doesn't take too long to make up his mind. *(Changing tone.)* Good evening.

Moctezuma Peon and his Assistant leave the rest rooms and cross the Cantina. Before leaving, Moctezuma Peon says a few words to Waitress Antonia, confidentially, and gives her something which could well be a tiny envelope of cocaine or a folded bill. Moctezuma Peon and his Assistant disappear into the street.

Pepe stays in the rest room a few moments, disconcerted, looking at the card. A customer enters and prepares to urinate, bringing Pepe to his senses. He leaves the rest rooms and goes to the domino table. During the time Pepe was in the rest rooms, his friends have finished the game. Efren has gone, his chair empty. Pepe reaches the table and occupies the chair. Ric mixes the pieces up again before choosing seven of them.

RIC: OK, let's see. Now, my dear Pepe, we're really gonna stick it to these mother fuckers.

Dalila peers briefly into the Cantina. She disappears. At the table where the game of dominoes is going on, the four reporters select pick their pieces. They arrange them. Pepe continues to be distracted.

PEPE: *(To Juan Jose)* Did you see those guys who just left?
JUAN JOSE: *(Looking toward the door)* What guys?
PEPE: Two guys. One was wearing a light colored suit. Tall. Big guy.
TOÑO: I didn't see anybody.
JUAN JOSE: Me neither. Why?
PEPE: No reason.

Ric throws a domino on to the table.

RIC: The six starts!

SCENE 4

Week 1. Tuesday afternoon. Between 3:30 and 4:30 p.m. It's about to rain.

Main action: Space 4: The Street

Simultaneous actions

Space 1: News room

Seated at Efren's desk, the Errand Boy is painstakingly typing, as if he were just learning. Ric, at his desk, has a writer's block: several times he gets up, feels around in a nearby desk until he finds a flask and takes a drink; he takes off his shirt to work in his undershirt; he paces back and forth, sits down again and begins to type. . . There are no other reporters in the News room. Shortly after the scene begins, Sagrario, the Managing Editor of the Newspaper arrives. She has just had lunch with the High Official, after their tour. It takes just one signal from Sagrario to make the Errand Boy come running to follow her into the Office. The Editor disappears into her private office, and we will see the Errand Boy come out with a pile of documents which he will start to photocopy, while Ric is still struggling with his writing.

Space 3: Cantina

Juan Jose and the Bartender are playing dice at the bar. The Waitress cleans up the tables people have left and then approaches Toño's table; he has been drinking alone. She sits down and talks with him.

Space 5: The Casablanca Club

Pato the Masseur has finished giving Agent 2 a massage; the latter is parsimoniously dressing.

Space 6: Government Offices

A little way into this scene (at the same time the Managing Editor enters the News room) High Official arrives at the empty offices with her entourage: Low Official and Assistants A and B. After them comes the Shoeshine Boy, who proceeds to polish Low Official's shoes in his office. High Official, on the other hand, orders her assistants not to bother her and prepares to take a nap on the sofa. She strips down to her underwear, puts on a Japanese robe, takes out a pillow and lies down.

Space 7: Taco Restaurant

The Taco Seller prepares tacos for some customers, who are eating voraciously. After they leave, The Taco Seller begins sharpening his knives. He does it expertly, showing a certain fascination with the instruments.

Space 8: Gerda's House

Gerda is seated in front of her television set, eating on a folding table. At the close of the scene Salcido will arrive. Agent 1 will be discreetly following him down the street.

Space 4: The Street.

The corner near the flower stand and the telephone booth.

The Neighbor is using the public telephone.

NEIGHBOR: *(Into the phone)* But he's not the child's father, Guadalupe; he's not the father and what he was doing is just plain kidnapping, if you want to know the truth. That's what all the fuss was about. They'd already warned him.

NEIGHBOR: No. What happened was, when they got home from work and couldn't find the kid, well, imagine, all hell broke loose. They went to Merceditas', then to Jimenez', because at first they thought he might be at the restaurant, you know how sometimes Jimenez entertains him with the stuff he's got there. But no. He wasn't anywhere. Moses had taken him away. It was clear as anything. Everybody knew it. That was when...

NEIGHBOR: That's right. Yeah. That was when they called the police and the ruckus started, 'cause the wife started to scream bloody murder and Guacho was insisting they call...

The Neighbor turns her back to us and gets closer to the telephone so that her conversation will be more private, at the same time that two people come toward the telephone. They are Pepe and Rosamaria. They cross the street and stop when Pepe notices the phone.

PEPE: Wait here just a minute. I'm going to call Juanito Miranda because later I won't be able to catch him and we'll end up with no photos. Why should I make more trouble for myself with Camacho?
ROSAMARIA: It's about to rain.

Pepe waits for the phone, ever more impatiently. The Neighbor keeps talking, but is now hunched over, so that we cannot hear her.

Space 5: The Club

When Agent 2 is finished dressing Salcido arrives. Agent 2 sees him and, afraid Salcido will find him, runs out brusquely. Salcido hardly notices him. Pato the Masseur is surprised, since Agent 2 left without paying.

PATO: Hey, hey you!

Pato runs after him but doesn't catch him. He returns in a bad mood.

PATO: That jerk. He stiffed me. I can't believe it.
SALCIDO: *(Paying no attention, preoccupied)* Do me a favor, Pato. Take this message over to the newspaper offices. Now.

PATO: Right now?
SALCIDO: Give it to a Mr. Gutierrez. Make sure you see he gets it in his own hands. That's very important: in his own hands. . . OK?
PATO: OK, sure.
SALCIDO: Thanks, Pato. *(He pats him on the back. He's about to leave.)* Oh, and another thing. You haven't seen me.

Salcido leaves the Club. For a moment Pato the Masseur doesn't move. Then he puts on his jacket and leaves quickly.

ROSAMARIA: Who else did you tell?
PEPE: About what?
ROSAMARIA: About this. About this mess you're in.
PEPE: Nobody else, just you and Juan Jose. . .You're the only one who knows about this morning and about what happened in the bar.
ROSAMARIA: Aren't you scared?

Pepe shakes his head, dubious

ROSAMARIA: The next time it's not just going to be a beating, Pepe. For that guy to be talking about eighty thousand dollars, this is serious stuff. Do you know what eighty thousand dollars is?
PEPE: All the money in the world.
ROSAMARIA: There you go. *(Transition.)* Why don't you talk to Camacho, Pepe? Or to Sagrario--once and for all.
PEPE: Not a chance.
ROSAMARIA: Let the paper back you. Protect you.
PEPE: No way.
ROSAMARIA: Well I'm starting to feel afraid. . .

Short silence. Pepe acts impatient for the Neighbor to finish. She is still hunched over the phone, her back to him.

PEPE: *(Discreetly, to Rosamaria)* This old hag is never gonna get off.

Space 6: Government Offices

The telephone in Low Official's office has rung. He answers and interrupts the shoeshine in order to go to his boss' office. After tapping on the door and receiving no answer, he opens the door and enters. High Official is sleeping. Low Official wakes her, shaking her gently.

LOW OFFICIAL: Mrs. Magaña... Mrs. Magaña...

High Official opens her eyes and raises up slightly.

LOW OFFICIAL: Captain Osorio's on the phone.
HIGH OFFICIAL: I told you not to wake me up, Cantu, you asshole!
LOW OFFICIAL: But there's been trouble... five dead.
HIGH OFFICIAL: Even if there were five thousand, God damn it! Let me rest... Don't bother me unless it's the network, just like I said!
LOW OFFICIAL: My apologies, Mrs. Magaña...

Low Official returns to his office and whispers something inaudible into the phone. He hangs up and leaves the office, clearly in a bad mood. The only people left in the Low Official's office are Assistants A and B, with the Shoeshine Boy. At this point the assistants begin to play sadistic games with the Shoeshine Boy. By the end of the scene they are playing Russian roulette with him, placing a pistol in his mouth and forcing him to pull the trigger. They do this twice; the Shoeshine Boy is terrified.

Space 5: Cantina

The conversation between Waitress Antonia and Toño has reached a climax.

TOÑO: So how much of a feel did that jerk get?
ANTONIA: What? Who do you mean? When?
TOÑO: The massage guy from the club.
ANTONIA: Nobody was feeling me up.
TOÑO: So what was it I saw?

ANTONIA: You saw wrong. I'm working. Or maybe you'd like to give me money to eat? To pay the rent?
TOÑO: You trying to say something?
ANTONIA: Just that. And if the one who needs the dough is you, well, just ask me for it. Go ahead! And cut the crap!

They continue their argument until the end of the scene, while the Bartender and Juan Jose are throwing dice.

ROSAMARIA: I'm leaving now. It's starting to sprinkle and Leticia said she'd be there at four. . . Are you going back to the office from here?
PEPE: No. Not til tonight.
ROSAMARIA: What time?
PEPE: Nine or nine thirty. But don't tell Calvo. . . I'll call you before that to see if there's any news from Salcido.

Pepe starts to leave, gesturing good-bye, but Rosamaria comes to him and forces him to kiss her on the mouth. Rosamaria prolongs the kiss. They separate. Rosamaria smiles.

ROSAMARIA: Bye.

Rosamaria opens her umbrella and goes off down the street. Pepe watches her for a moment and then turns impatiently to the Neighbor. She turns toward him but doesn't hang up. She is listening to the other person speak. The Neighbor looks at Pepe, sees his impatience and makes a signal meaning "just a minute." Neither Pepe nor the Neighbor seems to recognize the other from the brief encounter they had the day before in the building.

NEIGHBOR: *(Into the phone)*

--Well, sure.

--Well, sure.

Pepe gestures to the Neighbor that the situation is urgent. She turns her back to him and hunches over the phone to say something. Pepe looks at his watch with growing impatience. It takes him a moment to recognize Dalila who, wrapped in a raincoat, has come up to him slowly.

DALILA: *(Referring to Rosamaria)* Was that your wife?
PEPE: What are you doing here?
DALILA: Your lover? Your girlfriend? She's beautiful.
PEPE: What are you doing here?
DALILA: I've been following you all day. . . You were at the office until eleven thirty. From two to two thirty you were in the Cantina. From three to four you ate at VIPS, with that girl. Later the two of you went walking and ended up here.
PEPE: Why are you following me? Have you heard from Salcido?
DALILA: Because I love you.
PEPE: Have you heard from Salcido? Have you talked to him?
DALILA: To Chano?
PEPE: I've got to seem him. It's important.

Dalila smiles slightly and takes from a handbag a small manila envelope, which she hands to Pepe.

PEPE: What's this?

Dalila shrugs her shoulders. Pepe rips the envelope open anxiously and takes out a small gold key. He looks at it.

PEPE: What's this?
DALILA: *(Smiling)* A key.
PEPE: Did Salcido give it to you? Did he tell you to give it to me? Did you talk to him? *(He examines the envelope as if he hoped to find something else. There's nothing.)* How could he just send me this with no note, no explanation? *(Anxious. To Dalila)*: What's this about? What do you know?
DALILA: I don't know anything.
PEPE: What time did you talk to Salcido?
DALILA: Chano's going to call you, at your office, tonight. At ten sharp. He'll explain everything.
PEPE: Explain what?
DALILA: Everything. . . at ten sharp. He hopes you can be there at ten sharp. To make an appointment.
PEPE: To make an appointment or to explain everything?
DALILA: To make an appointment and explain everything.
PEPE: About this key. . .
DALILA: About everything.

PEPE: Is that what he told you?

Without answering, Dalila stares at Pepe, sweetly. They kiss.

DALILA: I love you.

Silence.

PEPE: You know Salcido pretty well, don't you? Chano.
DALILA: Yes.
PEPE: Does he live with you? On Serapio Rendon?
DALILA: Sometimes.
PEPE: What do you mean, "sometimes?" Do you mean sometimes he's there and sometimes he's not?

Dalila nods her head "yes."

PEPE: Is he your husband?

Dalila shakes her head "no."

PEPE: Are you and he lovers?
DALILA: Yes. You could say we're lovers. . . We sleep together. We make love, like you and I did, yesterday. *(Long pause.)* We're also brother and sister.
PEPE: Salcido's your brother. . . and your lover?
DALILA: *(Smiling)* Yes.

The Neighbor finishes her telephone call. Before coming out of the booth, she looks at Pepe. At that moment she seems to remember that he's the same man she saw the previous day, in the building. She seems disconcerted.

NEIGHBOR: Excuse me, but it was a matter of life and death.

The Neighbor comes out, but doesn't completely disappear from sight. From a distance, near the flower stand, she watches Pepe and Dalila. Also at her stand, the Florist has not taken her eyes off of the scene taking place in front of the telephone booth. Likewise Moctezuma Peon's Assistant, though from a greater distance. He has been fascinated by Pepe's two love scenes.

No One Knows Anything 47

Disconcerted by what Dalila has just told him, Pepe goes to the phone, picks up the receiver, wipes off the sweat the Neighbor has left on it and is about to dial.

DALILA: Are you coming to see me tonight, after you talk to Chano? I have some new poems.
PEPE: By Concha Urquiza.
DALILA: Love poems.

Dalila smiles and walks away. Pepe dials a number. Thunder announces an imminent rain.

Space 1: News room

Ric, in his undershirt, restless, getting up and down, is typing. At the photocopy machine, Errand Boy is making copies of the papers that the Managing Editor gave him. Pato the Masseur arrives. Ric waits on him, since he is the nearest to the entrance.

RIC: What can I do for you?
PATO THE MASSEUR: I'm looking for Mr. Gutierrez.
RIC: Yes?
PATO THE MASSEUR: Are you Mr. Gutierrez?
RIC: No, but what can I do for you?
PATO THE MASSEUR: Do you know what time he'll be in?
RIC: *(To the Errand Boy)* What time's Pepe supposed to come in?
ERRAND BOY: Who knows!
RIC: *(To Pato)* We don't know.
PATO THE MASSEUR: Do you know if he's coming in?
RIC: *(To the Errand Boy)* Is he coming in?
ERRAND BOY: Who knows?
RIC: *(To Pato)* Who knows? Can I help you?
PATO THE MASSEUR: I have an envelope for him.
RIC: I can give it to him if you want.
PATO THE MASSEUR: It's personal.
RIC: I can still give it to him. What's the problem?
PATO THE MASSEUR: It's personal.
RIC: So what's the problem?
PATO THE MASSEUR: I don't know.
RIC: *(Acting bothered, he says to himself as he walks off)* Well, you can eat shit... *(To the Errand Boy:)* You take care of this guy, OK?

The Errand Boy comes up to Pato the Masseur.

ERRAND BOY: Well?
PATO: I have an envelope for Mr. Gutierrez.
ERRAND BOY: Sure. I'll put it in his mailbox.
PATO: I'm supposed to hand it to him personally.
ERRAND BOY: He'll get it, mister.
PATO: I can't just leave it there.
ERRAND BOY: Don't worry. That's where everybody leaves their messages for the reporters.
PATO: We'll, I *am* worried.
ERRAND BOY: It won't get lost. Nothing gets lost around here.
PATO: But I was told to give it to him personally.
ERRAND BOY: If you don't trust us, don't leave it.
PATO: He'll get it today?
ERRAND BOY: If he comes today, he'll get it today.

Pato the Masseur gives him the envelope, doubting. The Errand Boy places it in Pepe's mailbox.

Dalila has gone over to the flower stand while Pepe makes his phone call. She takes a rose from a bouquet, goes to Pepe and gives it to him. A heavy rain begins to fall. Dalila, the Neighbor and Moctezuma Peon's Assistant begin to run. The Florist takes out a large multicolored umbrella to protect herself from the rain. Pepe continues to talk on the phone in the booth.

SCENE 5

Week 1. Tuesday night. Between 9:30 and 10:30 p.m. It is raining.

Main action: Space 1: News room

Simultaneous actions

Space 2: Apartment Building

Dalila is in her Apartment writing poems at the secretaire in the room. Chamber music can be heard.

The Neighbor comes out of her apartment with two large bags of garbage which she leaves, clandestinely, in a dark area on the street. She returns to her apartment and starts to pray before an image of the Sacred Heart. Later she turns out the lights.

Space 3:   Cantina

Toño is drinking, still seated at the table he occupied during the previous scene. At the bar, while the Shoeshine Boy cleans his shoes, Low Official drinks martinis the Bartender mixes, following Moctezuma Peon's instructions. Waitress Antonia waits on the many tables occupied at that hour.

Space 6:   Government Offices

Having put on her tailored suit again, High Official looks over some papers. She is unhappy that neither Low Official nor Assistants A and B are in the Office. She keeps looking in vain for them in Low Official's office.

Space 7:   Taco Restaurant

The Taco Seller is extremely busy serving his customers. Agent 2 and Efren Malvido are there, conversing.

Space 8:   Gerda's House

Gerda is in front of the television set. She is watching the screen attentively but continually changes the channel with the remote control.

Outside the house Agent 1 stands guard.

Space 9:   Cabaret

The tables and the dance floor are full of customers. Very late, with the loud multicolored umbrella she had in the previous scene, the Florist arrives at the Cabaret: she works here by night as a call girl. She disappears for a moment and then reappears dressed already in keeping with the place. Moctezuma Peon's Assistant, who arrives in the

> *company of his boss Moctezuma Peon, begins dancing with her. Moctezuma Peon takes a seat at a corner table and orders a bottle of whiskey and glasses.*

The News room is intensely busy. Except for Pepe's and Efren's places, all the desks are occupied by reporters who work feverishly. The Errand Boy goes from one to another picking up materials and taking them to the Managing Editor's Office. Rosamaria, at her desk, answers telephone calls or helps some of the reporters.

JUAN JOSE: *(From his desk, calling)* Gofer!
ERRAND BOY: At your service, be right there!

The Errand Boy goes to Juan Jose. Juan Jose gives him a few pages.

JUAN JOSE: Tell her this is the next to last. Just three more pages and that's it.
RIC: *(From his desk)* Gofer!
ERRAND BOY: I'm coming!
RIC: Get me last Thursday's *Excelsior*, please.
JUAN JOSE: Hurry up with those pages.
RIC: The *Excelsior*.
ERRAND BOY: Hold on, I can't be in twenty places at once.
RIC: Stinking faggot.

The Errand Boy disappears and reappears. Everyone is working intensely.

> **Space 8: Gerda's House**
>
> *Pato the Masseur arrives at Gerda's house. The old woman opens the door.*
>
> **PATO:** Good evening, Mrs. Gerda. Is Lorenzo home?
> **GERDA:** He's sick.
> **PATO:** He wanted to see me. It's urgent. He's expecting some news from me.
> **GERDA:** Well, let me see.
>
> *Gerda disappears into a back room. Salcido enters, wearing a bathrobe, hair uncombed.*

PATO: I delivered your message, sir.
SALCIDO: Personally?
PATO: Not exactly... He wasn't there. I went to the newspaper and he wasn't there. I left it there. They said he'd get it anyway, today.
SALCIDO: I asked you to give it to him personally.
PATO: But he wasn't there, sir.

Salcido shakes his head. They exchange a few more words and then Pato retires. Gerda comes into the room and continues to watch television. Salcido accompanies her until the end of the scene, but he seems more involved with his own thoughts than with the screen. From time to time, Gerda extends her hand and caresses her son's head.

Pepe enters the News room, his raincoat soaked. He comes to Rosamaria's desk.

ROSAMARIA: Did you get wet?
PEPE: It's raining like hell out there. Jesus!
ROSAMARIA: Just look at you.
PEPE: *(While he shakes off water and takes his raincoat off)* Any news from Salcido? He didn't call?
ROSAMARIA: Not a word.
PEPE: Are you sure?
ROSAMARIA: Positive. I've been here the whole time.
PEPE: He's gonna call me at ten sharp on 47. Don't let anybody use that line, OK? I don't want it blocked.
ROSAMARIA: It's gonna be hard to reserve it, at that time of night.
PEPE: Even if it is, try. Try hard.

Ric laughs.

Space 6:   Government Offices

Assistant A and Assistant B have just arrived and High Official surprises them in the office of Low Official, who is still in the Cantina. High Official reprimands the Assistants:

> **HIGH OFFICIAL:** Don't let this happen again, do you hear me? *(To Assistant B:)* And you, why are you wearing those glasses? Take them off!

Assistant takes his dark glasses off.

> **HIGH OFFICIAL:** Sorry, sorry, put them back on. *(Transition.)* Let's get this clear, once and for all: you all are here to carry out to the letter whatever your superiors order. . . That's why you're here and not back in the barracks. To follow orders, is that clear? To follow orders. *(Pause. To Assistant A:)* Come with me, Augusto, come over here.

> *High Official goes into her office, followed by Assistant A. It appears that she is scolding him again in the office. She gives him several assignments that he and Assistant A will try to carry out in the office of Low Official. They look for papers, make telephone calls, etc.*

Pepe crosses the News room and stops in front of Juan Jose's desk.

PEPE: How're you doing with that?
JUAN JOSE: Just finishing the first one. I've still got two to go.
PEPE: Do you know if Juanito Miranda brought the pictures of Uruchurtu?
JUAN JOSE: Yeah. He told me he gave them to Camacho.
PEPE: What do you mean he gave them to Camacho? Why didn't he wait for me?
JUAN JOSE: It looked like he was in a hurry.
PEPE: Are they from the archives?
JUAN JOSE: I don't think so. He's unrecognizable. *(Transition).* Camacho wanted to see you. He really needed your interview with Corona del Rosal. . . How was it?
PEPE: OK, I guess. . . Stupid idiot, likes to hear himself talk.

Pepe looks at his watch. He goes to his typewriter, sits.

> **Space 3: Cantina**
>
> *Low Official has continued drinking at the bar of the Cantina while the Shoeshine Boy shines his shoes. Low Official, very drunk already, caresses the boy's head several times and then shows him several dollar bills. He smiles at him and takes him to the rest room. There, the*

> *Shoeshine Boy kneels before him and performs fellatio. The Shoeshine Boy takes the dollars and leaves the Cantina running. He spits as he goes. Low Official also leaves the cantina, after tossing down one more martini at the bar. He leaves a generous tip for the Bartender.*

Juan Jose goes to Pepe's desk.

JUAN JOSE: Hey, your lead's turning serious, isn't it?
PEPE: What?
JUAN JOSE: That guy from the bar. Rosamaria told me.
PEPE: What did she tell you?
JUAN JOSE: About that guy. The one who offered you money for Salcido's papers. That jerk.
PEPE: And why did Rosamaria tell you about that?
JUAN JOSE: Well, she knows that you and I . . . *(Transition:)* It bugs you that she told me, doesn't it, Pepe? Tell me, does it bother you? Huh?
PEPE: Well, no, but. . .
JUAN JOSE: She thought the whole thing was bizarre. She was worried about you. Me too.
PEPE: Yeah, yeah, OK.
JUAN JOSE: We can talk about it later, if you want.
PEPE: Sure.
JUAN JOSE: Don't get mad.
PEPE: I'm not mad.

The telephone rings. Pepe reacts anxiously, because he's waiting for Salcido's call on that line.

ROSAMARIA: *(Into the phone)*
--News room.
−
--Chabelita?
−
--Oh, yeah, Chabelita. I already sent it over, with the Errand Boy.
−
--Sure, Chabelita.
−
--Sure, Chabelita.

--Chabelita, can I call you back in about fifteen minutes? I'm expecting a very important call on this line.

--Of course not, Chabelita.

--Seriously, Chabelita.

--Yes, yes.

--Yes, Chabelita, I'll call you in fifteen minutes.

She hangs up, resumes activity. The phone rings.

ROSAMARIA: *(Into the phone)*
--News room.

--Chabelita!

--Chabelita, come on, I said I'd call you in fifteen minutes.

--Yeah.

--I won't forget, really.

--Yes, Chabelita.

Pepe comes over. He grabs the receiver away from Rosamaria and hangs it up himself. Pause.

PEPE: You didn't ask me if you could tell Juan Jose.
ROSAMARIA: What's that?
PEPE: You told him about the guy in the bar.
ROSAMARIA: Oh. . . Sorry. *(Pause.)* I'm sorry, Pepe, I did it because. . .
PEPE: Since when are you so close to him?
ROSAMARIA: I'm sorry. It won't happen again. . . I didn't think you'd mind. I didn't think, I guess.

Pepe makes a vague gesture of disgust and, distractedly, looks through the contents of his mailbox. He is surprised to find a manila envelope, identical to the one Dalila gave him in the telephone booth.

PEPE: *(Looking at the envelope, then at Rosamaria)* Who brought this?

ROSAMARIA: What? *(Sees the envelope)* Oh, I don't know. It wasn't there when I got here. I looked in your box and there was nothing there. They didn't give it to me.

Pepe opens the envelope and reads a small card. The Errand Boy is crossing the room. Rosamaria stops him.

ROSAMARIA: Hey. . . Did you put that envelope in Pepe's mailbox?
ERRAND BOY: Yeah, why?
PEPE: Who brought it?
ERRAND BOY: Some guy came in and gave it to me. Around five. And I put it in your box.
PEPE: What guy?
ERRAND BOY: An ordinary sort of guy. I'd never seen him before. . . He was wearing a running suit.
PEPE: What'd he say to you?
ERRAND BOY: Nothing. He gave it to me and that was it. And I put it in your mailbox.

Pepe makes a gesture meaning "OK" and the Errand Boy goes back to his work. Pepe rereads, to himself, what is written on the card.

ROSAMARIA: Is it from Salcido?

Pepe nods.

ROSAMARIA: What does it say?
PEPE: Nothing. *(Pause:)* He says we can talk tomorrow, at seven in the morning.
ROSAMARIA: Seven in the morning?

Pepe walks away from Rosamaria and talks, in the distance, with Juan Jose.

PEPE: Hey, Juan Jose, do you know where the Casablanca Club is?
JUAN JOSE: The Casablanca Club? No idea.

From his desk, without interrupting his typing, Ric responds.

RIC: Right near here, around Paris street. On the other side of Reforma. They give massages there.

PEPE: Is it private or public?
RIC: Private, I think. For quite a while now.

Space 9: Cabaret

Moctezuma Peon's Assistant has been dancing with the Florist. She quits dancing and goes to the Waiter. She speaks with him. The Waiter disappears and reappears carrying a covered tray which he places in front of Moctezuma Peon, on the table. The Shoeshine Boy is present, with his shoeshine box.

WAITER: Here you are, boss.

The Waiter leaves, Moctezuma Peon uncovers the tray and reveals a package. He opens it (it appears to contain cocaine) and tests the quality of the merchandise by pressing some on to his finger tip and spreading it on to his gums. Moctezuma stores a smaller package in one of his pockets; after folding the original package in two, he places it in the Shoeshine Boy's box.

MOCTEZUMA PEON: *(To the Shoeshine Boy)* This is the fifth of the month. Don't forget it. *(Pause.)* Or you'll pay with your life, you stupid mute.

The Shoeshine boy nods. He closes his box and disappears. Moctezuma Peon and his Assistant stay in the Cabaret until the end of the scene.

The reporters in the News room continue their work. The telephone rings. Rosamaria responds:

Simultaneous scenes

From Space 7: Taco Restaurant. Efren Malvido has been talking with Agent 2. He gets up to go to a nearby telephone booth. He dials. Rosamaria, at the News room, answers.

ROSAMARIA: *(Into the phone)* Good afternoon. News room.
EFREN: Put Pepe on, Rosi. Quick.
ROSAMARIA: Who's calling?

EFREN: Efren, Rosi. Hurry.

Rosamaria gets Pepe's attention.

ROSAMARIA: Telephone, Pepe... Efren. Says it's very important.

Pepe goes to the phone.

PEPE: Gutierrez.
EFREN: It's me, Pepe, Efren. Listen... Something's come up, I'm not gonna be able to get to the office tonight, but I've got to talk to you. It's urgent. I need your help.
PEPE: Right now? I'm right in the middle of...
EFREN: No, no, tomorrow morning, if you can. We can have breakfast.
PEPE: I've got an appointment.
EFREN: What time?
PEPE: Early.
EFREN: What time?
PEPE: Very early. At seven.
EFREN: Oh, well, we could get together afterwards. Is your appointment far?
PEPE: No, near here.
EFREN: Where?
PEPE: Near here, somewhere near Paris street.
EFREN: OK, that's fine. I'll see you after your appointment. It's really important, pal, I'll be forever grateful... How about if we meet at Sanborn's at Lafragua, say, about nine?
PEPE: I don't know if I can make it. I don't know how long I'll be.
EFREN: Nine or nine thirty.
PEPE: I'm just not sure.
EFREN: Well, I'll be waiting there anyway... If you can't make it, call the restaurant. Ask for Tommy, you know him. It's really important, Pepe.
PEPE: OK.
EFREN: Thanks, pal. Thanks.

Pepe hangs up the phone. Efren leaves the phone booth and returns to the Taco Restaurant, to Agent 2, who has been watching the telephone scene from afar.

EFREN: *(To Agent 2)* It's in the Casablanca, all right. At seven.

Pepe returns to his desk. The reporters type.

RIC: Gofer! Last Thursday's *Excelsior*, please.
JUAN JOSE: Gofer!

Space 3: Cantina

In the Cantina, Toño is suffering from a sudden attack of fury. He gets up from his table and starts to throw everything onto the floor, to deliver insults, to protest. With the help of several customers, the Bartender manages to grab him and throw him into the street, like a sack of potatoes. The Waitress Antonia goes out after him. She finds him on the ground, vomiting, crying. She cleans him up, caresses him, helps him get to his feet.

SCENE 6

Week 1. Wednesday morning. 7 a.m.

Main action: Space 5: The Casablanca Club

Simultaneous actions

Space 1: News room

The Errand Boy, who sleeps every night in the News room because his family lives far from the city, is waking up. He folds his blankets and pad and puts them away, as always, between two desks. He prepares himself a cup of coffee. He goes into the rest rooms to wash up. He returns.

Space 2: Apartment Building

On the roof of the Apartment Building, as if hallucinating, Dalila is reciting poems. She gives the impression of having been there all night, awaiting with her poetry the tragic events which are about to occur.

Space 4: The Street

Waitress Antonia emerges from a car and walks away. The occupant of the car blows the horn, calling to her. Waitress Antonia returns to the car and takes a scarf she had forgotten. She stops at a stand to drink some atole.

Efren crosses the street holding his son's hand. He is taking him to school.

Low Official is waking up. He has fallen asleep on a park bench. He is still drunk, disheveled, dirty. He sits up and fumbles with a small envelope of cocaine. He "snorts" some of the drug, which revives him. He disappears down the street.

The Florist reaches her flower stand still dressed as a call girl. At the stand she changes clothes and begins to prepare the stand.

People who cross the street: people out exercising, passersby who buy papers at the news stand, people on bicycles. . .

Space 6: Government Offices

Assistant B is in High Official's Office, furtively installing a hidden microphone in her private telephone.

Space 8: Gerda's House

Gerda is giving the Shoeshine Boy an airmail envelope so he can take it to the post office. The Shoeshine Boy takes his tip and goes out into the street. He has scarcely left the building when he opens the envelope, takes out some dollar bills the envelope contained, and tosses the letter somewhere.

Space 5: The Casablanca Club.
In an area near the dressing rooms, a naked man lies face down on a table. Pato the Masseur is giving him a massage, energetically and with good technique.

Agent 1 undresses in front of the lockers and goes into the steam room. Agent 2, in a suit, hides between the lockers. Pato does not see him.

Salcido arrives. He greets Pato and talks to him in a low voice, at length. Then he undresses, puts his clothes in a locker and goes into the steam room. Inside, where there are four or five customers, Salcido thinks he recognizes Agent 1. Nervous, he comes out quickly, but at the door he is confronted by Agent 2, who points a pistol at him and forces him to go in again. Salcido obeys. Pato the Masseur is oblivious to the whole scene, busy with his work.

Toño is one of the customers inside the area of the steam room. He is very hungover. He comes out and goes to where Pato is working.

TOÑO: How 'bout a beer, Pato? This hangover's killing me.
PATO: How much do you owe me?
TOÑO: Nothing. I'm paid up. Remember?
PATO: OK, take one.

Toño goes to where the beers are. He takes two and puts them in a bucket with ice.

TOÑO: Is this all the ice you have? It's frozen solid.

With an ice pick, Toño tries to break up the ice, which is preventing the beers from sliding into the bucket. He takes the bucket, with the beers, into the area of the steam room. He sits down next to Agent 1, who is watching a very nervous Salcido.

Pepe appears in the area of the dressing rooms, having come in from the street. He goes to Pato the Masseur.

PATO: Can I help you?
PEPE: I'm looking for a Mr. Salcido.
PATO: Who?
PEPE: Salcido. He told me to meet him here.

Pato the Masseur interrupts his work.

PATO: *(To the man on the table)* Excuse me just a minute. *(He goes toward Pepe, looks at him a moment.)* Are you Mr. Jose Gutierrez?
PEPE: That's me.
PATO: Newspaper reporter?

Pepe nods.

PATO: Salcido's in the steam room. He asked me to tell you to meet him in there, so you could talk comfortably. . . Unless, of course, you'd rather not.
PEPE: *(Disconcerted)* No. . .

Pato the Masseur gestures to Pepe to follow him and he takes him to an area in front of the lockers. He shows him a bench. . . From the inside of a locker he takes a couple of towels and gives them to him.

PATO: You can leave your clothes in here. *(He indicates an area)* The steam room is through that door.
PEPE: Thanks.

Pato the Masseur walks back to his table and resumes his massage. Pepe undresses slowly, slightly uncomfortable because of being in a strange place, in a strange situation. He folds his clothing carefully and places it on the bench. Then he changes his mind and puts the pile of clothes in the locker indicated by Pato pointed out to him. He closes the narrow locker door. Once undressed, Pepe wraps one of the towels around his waist and with the other in his hand he walks toward the area of the steam room. He goes in. He looks for a place. He takes a seat, expectantly.

PEPE: *(Raising his voice a little)* Salcido. . ?

Salcido, at the other end of the room, gets up. He tries to warn Pepe.

SALCIDO: Gutierrez. . .

When Salcido stands up, Agent 1 tries to stop him, to prevent him from reaching Gutierrez. Salcido struggles. Agent 1 gets nervous and, absurdly exasperated that Salcido is getting away from him, he automatically takes the ice pick from Toño's bucket, which is near him, and stabs Salcido with it once, then several more times.

Agent 1 runs out, naked. He joins Agent 2, who is shouting at him.

AGENT 2: You idiot!

Agent 1 and Agent 2 disappear. In the area of the steam room, Salcido falls to the ground. Shouts are heard, expressions of surprise. Salcido's blood bathes the white tiles of the place.

ACT TWO

SCENE 7

Week 2. Monday night. Between 10 and 11 p.m.

Main Action: Space 6: Government Offices

Simultaneous actions

Space 1:   News room

Intense activity in the News room. Only Juan Jose and Pepe are absent; the other reporters are working feverishly. It is obvious that Efren is in a bad mood. He continually throws into the waste paper basket crumpled pages of unsuccessful writing. The Errand Boy goes about his task of carrying notes to the Managing Editor's area. Rosamaria is also very busy; the Managing Editor calls her a couple of times.

Space 2:   Apartment Building

Pato the Masseur arrives at Dalila's apartment and opens it with a key. Then he begins casing the place, as he will do during the whole scene, as if he were a thief.

The Neighbor, in her apartment, is suffering from an attack of insomnia. She paces from room to room, takes pills, lights a votive candle to the Sacred Heart, stares at the street below from the window, where she remains for a long while with a sad, lost look on her face.

Space 3: Cantina

Most of the customers are watching a soccer game on the television.

Space 5: The Casablanca Club

Waitress Antonia, dressed as if she were a prostitute awaiting a client, waits in the area of the lockers. She has been drinking from a bottle she found there. She is obviously in a bad mood.

Space 7: Taco Restaurant

Few clients are in the small restaurant. The Taco Seller is tossing coins with the Shoeshine Boy, calling out "heads or tails?" The Shoeshine Boy almost always wins. The Taco Seller pays him with tacos which the Shoeshine Boy eats, happily.

Space 9: Cabaret

A whirl of activity on the dance floor. The Florist is the center of attention, an outstanding dancer. Toño is at a table, dancing.

Space 6: Government Offices.

In her private office, High Official is carefully examining some files. Assistant A is with her, paying close attention to what she is saying to him, especially to the orders she gives him. He is acting as a secretary.

Next door, in Low Official's Office, Pepe and Juan Jose are sitting, waiting. Down one hallway we can see Low Official accompanying Gerda toward the exit from the floor.

LOW OFFICIAL: *(To Gerda)* Let me repeat what Mrs. Magaña just said: it's all over. We won't be bothering you again.
GERDA: *(Interrupting him)* God help me! It was your policemen who turned my apartment upside down.
LOW OFFICIAL: I understand.
GERDA: You don't understand anything.

Low Official smiles understandingly and disappears for a moment with Gerda. Seconds later, Gerda comes out of the Government Offices accompanied by Dalila. They are both wearing black. They disappear down the street.

Space 1: News room

The reporters are still working. Rosamaria is in the Editor's office. The Errand Boy interrupts his coming and going for a moment to participate in the conversation between Ric and Efren. Ric is teasing Efren.
RIC: *(Apparently seriously)* It's all out, Efren.
EFREN: *(Suddenly worried)* What's out?
RIC: What you're up to.
EFREN: What am I up to?
ERRAND BOY: Come on, Efren, what do you think? Lupita's already called you twice.
EFREN: Oh, that. . .
RIC: What a temper she's got, huh?

Efren forces a smile. He goes back to work, but little by little the reporters leave, having finished their work. Toward the end of the scene we see Sagrario come out of her office, dressed with exaggerated elegance, as if she were going to a big party.

Finally the only ones left in the news room are: Ric, Efren, Errand Boy and Rosamaria.

Low Official returns to his office and sits down at his desk. He talks to Pepe and Juan Jose.

LOW OFFICIAL: *(Referring to Gerda)* Poor woman. *(Changing tone:)* You know her, don't you?

Pepe shakes his head "no."

LOW OFFICIAL: She's Salcido's mother.

Pepe looks surprised. Low Official notices his surprise. Silence. Low Official idly moves some papers and then turns to Pepe. (It is evident he is trying to speak and look at only Pepe.)

LOW OFFICIAL: OK, Gutierrez, my friend, I think we're finished now. Mrs. Magaña will speak with the managing editor of your paper and not one more line, not one more article. There won't be anymore interrogations or problems for you either. Are we clear?
PEPE: Perfectly clear.
JUAN JOSE: But the investigation of the crime will go on.
LOW OFFICIAL: I beg your pardon?
JUAN JOSE: The investigation of Salcido's murder will go on.
LOW OFFICIAL: Of course. Everything will follow its course, according to the law.
JUAN JOSE: But the agents of the law keep saying it was a crime of passion.
LOW OFFICIAL: The agents in charge of this case have more information than any of the rest of us. *(Quick transition.)* Before you leave, Mr. Gutierrez, let me see if Mrs. Magaña has a minute. She wanted to meet you, have a word with you. *(He picks up the receiver of his telephone and presses a button. He speaks into the phone.)* Silvino?
ASSISTANT A: *(Into the phone)* Yes, sir.
LOW OFFICIAL: *(Into the phone)* I'm here with Mr. Gutierrez... He would like to say hello to Mrs. Magaña. He won't take much of her time. He just wants a minute. See if it's possible, Silvino.
ASSISTANT A: *(Into the phone)* Just a minute. *(Covers the telephone and turns to High Official.)* Cantu says he's ready.
HIGH OFFICIAL: Tell them to come in.
ASSISTANT A: *(Into the phone)* You can come in.
LOW OFFICIAL: Thanks.

Low Official hangs up his phone and comes toward Pepe.

LOW OFFICIAL: Mrs. Magaña is ready for us, Mr. Gutierrez.

Pepe and Juan Jose rise at the same time.

LOW OFFICIAL: *(To Juan Jose)* Just Mr. Gutierrez, my friend. *(Pause.)* Would you mind waiting for us in the next room? I'd appreciate it.

Juan Jose smiles sarcastically and leaves the office through the door indicated by Low Official. The latter and Pepe enter the office of High

Official. At the moment she is talking on one of the phones on her desk. Assistant A is present. Low Official and Pepe stand back, waiting for her to finish.

LOW OFFICIAL: *(In a low tone, secretively)* Your friend is a hostile person.
PEPE: Do you think so?
LOW OFFICIAL: Very hostile... What does he do at the paper?
PEPE: He covers the labor stories.
LOW OFFICIAL: So that's it.
HIGH OFFICIAL: *(Into the phone)* That's right.

--That's right.

--That's right.

High Official notices the presence of Pepe and Low Official and, smiling, signals them to come closer and to take a seat in front of her. They obey.

--Perfectly.

High Official hangs up the phone. She takes a bundle of papers and hands it to Assistant A.

HIGH OFFICIAL: *(To Assistant A)* I want it in fifteen minutes. We have to be in the President's Office at 22:30.

Assistant A takes the bundle and leaves the office. High Official returns Pepe's gaze. She smiles broadly.

HIGH OFFICIAL: I'm delighted to meet you, Mr. Gutierrez. It really is a pleasure. I've been a faithful reader of your articles for a long time and believe me I admire you very much. I'll never forget that great article you published on the Laguna Verde situation... when was that? In April, I seem to recall ... Was it in April?
PEPE: Yes, it was in April.
HIGH OFFICIAL: A marvelous piece, really. Splendid research. Profound. One of those journalistic pieces that teach something to those of us who work in the public sector. Not at all sensational or sectarian. You all help us think and clear

up our ideas on the advantages and disadvantages of a nuclear plant of that magnitude. It's a tremendous problem for the Mexican government. Tremendous. *(Transition.)* Did you read his article on Laguna Verde, Joaquin?
LOW OFFICIAL: Unfortunately no, Mrs. Magaña.
HIGH OFFICIAL: Well, you should read it. It's a paragon of journalistic research. Tell Augusto to make you a copy. I've got it in my files.

Space 2: Apartment Building; Space 5: Club

Pato the Masseur has continued his mysterious search in Dalila's apartment. Suddenly he seems to remember something and he makes a telephone call.

The phone rings in the Casablanca Club, where Antonia is waiting, inebriated by now. She picks up the receiver.

WAITRESS: *(Into the phone)* Helloooo...
PATO: *(Into the phone)* Antonia... Is that you, Antonia?
WAITRESS: What do you want?
PATO: I'm really sorry, Toña. This is Pato. Something came up and my customers canceled out. They're not coming.
WAITRESS: You made me wait all this time? I've been here four hours!
PATO: I'm sorry, Toña, it's just that...
WAITRESS: *(Hanging up abruptly)* Go to hell!

Antonia furiously attacks her surroundings. She throws a bottle of beer, breaking a glass case containing numerous jars of lotion. Then she continues drinking.

In Dalila's apartment, Pato continues his search, assisted by a flashlight.

HIGH OFFICIAL: You have my sincere congratulations, Mr. Gutierrez.
PEPE: Thank you. Thank you very much.

HIGH OFFICIAL: I wanted to meet you and tell you this personally... Unfortunately our work doesn't usually allow us to congratulate the journalists who carry out their mission of truthfully and accurately informing the public... But when the opportunity does arise, I like to take it. And I'm taking it now, Mr. Gutierrez. Believe me, I'm absolutely sincere.
PEPE: Thank you, Mrs. Magaña.
HIGH OFFICIAL: About that other matter. I imagine Cantu has briefed you on our position.
PEPE: That's right.
LOW OFFICIAL: Mr. Gutierrez is completely informed and is ready to cooperate with us fully.
HIGH OFFICIAL: I'm infinitely grateful. And confidentially, Mr. Gutierrez. Let me just tell you confidentially that those documents were taken directly from the President's office. Do you know what that means?
PEPE: Yes, yes I do.

Space 3: Cantina

The customers are cheering for a play in the soccer game they are watching. They shout at the same time as the announcer.

CUSTOMERS: Goal!!!!

HIGH OFFICIAL: State Secret. A matter of national security. Naturally everything's under control and there is absolutely no chance of infiltrators, but we wouldn't want there to be more deaths or extraordinary conflicts... That's why I am so grateful and indebted to you for your inclination to cooperate with us and I trust we'll hear from you in the very near future.

Suddenly High Official stands, forcing Pepe and Low Official to stand as well.

HIGH OFFICIAL: Mr. Gutierrez, it's been a pleasure talking to you. I'm honored to make your acquaintance. *(Aside, to Low Official)*: Call them!

Quickly, Low Official exits through a rear door of the office and disappears. High Official directs Pepe to leave through the door through which he entered the office.

HIGH OFFICIAL: I'm here to serve you. We'll be seeing each other soon, I hope. *(Extends her hand to him.)*
PEPE: *(Shaking High Official's hand)* Good-bye, Mrs. Magaña. Thank you very much.

Visibly shaken, Pepe finds himself once again in the office of Low Official. He sees Assistants A and B going quickly into High Official's Office. Pepe remains in the office a few moments, not knowing what to do. Low Official arrives.

LOW OFFICIAL: Quite a lady, isn't she? I told you. That's why I was so interested in you meeting her personally.
PEPE: Thank you.
LOW OFFICIAL: I'm here to serve you, too, Mr. Gutierrez, for whatever you might need. Don't forget what we've said today.
PEPE: Of course not.

Pepe is about to leave. Low Official stops him, at the last minute.

LOW OFFICIAL: Oh, I almost forgot. A technical question... Mrs. Magaña has set aside a sum of money, a considerable sum, to . . . how should we put it? As an expression of gratitude for whatever information might turn up about the whereabouts of those papers. You understand. No one who decides to cooperate with us will be disappointed. In these cases the government--and especially Mrs. Magaña--is very generous, Mr. Gutierrez. *(He extends his hand. Shakes Pepe's hand.)* Good-bye.

Pepe disappears through the door to the office. Low Official returns to High Official's office, where High Official is with Assistants A and B. High Official is staring at some papers. She makes them all wait, expectantly.

Space 1:   News room

Only Efren, Rosamaria and Ric are still in the News room. While Efren writes, Ric has gone to Rosamaria's desk and has been talking to her at length as if he wanted somehow to seduce her. Rosamaria has been smiling at him.

RIC: Hey, Efren. . . I've got to go now. I promised I'd take Rosamaria home and. . . Can you wait around til Galarza gets here?
EFREN: What time's Galarza supposed to get here?
RIC: He shouldn't be long. Ten minutes at the most. . . Just til he comes? Cover for me?
EFREN: OK, I'll stay.

Ric smiles at him gratefully and he and Rosamaria leave the building. Efren continues writing.

High Official takes her eyes from her papers and talks alternately with Assistant A and Assistant B.

HIGH OFFICIAL: Don't let them get out of your sight. Make them understand I'm absolutely serious about this. When I say "enough" I mean "enough"! *(Pause.)* Is that clear?
ASSISTANT A: Totally clear, Mrs. Magaña.

Assistant A and Assistant B leave High Official's office.

LOW OFFICIAL: What should I do with Moctezuma Peon?
HIGH OFFICIAL: Is he here?
LOW OFFICIAL: He's been waiting upstairs about a half hour.
HIGH OFFICIAL: Tell him I don't have anything to say to him. . . He's out of this now. Now it's up to us and I don't want him in the way.
LOW OFFICIAL: He's furious.
HIGH OFFICIAL: That's his problem.

Low Official returns to his office. Moctezuma Peon is already there, nervous, excited.

MOCTEZUMA PEON: Is she finally gonna see me?
LOW OFFICIAL: Mrs. Magaña asked me to tell you again, Mr. Moctezuma, that you are to withdraw from the case because the case is now exclusively ours.
MOCTEZUMA PEON: I don't receive my orders from Mrs. Magaña. She's not my boss.
LOW OFFICIAL: She has the sole responsibility for. . .

MOCTEZUMA PEON: *(Interrupting)* Don't be ridiculous! Doesn't she understand? I get my orders directly from the President's office and no cabinet member can go above that.
LOW OFFICIAL: You're the one who doesn't understand the situation, Mr. Moctezuma.
MOCTEZUMA PEON: From the beginning this office promised to collaborate with me.
LOW OFFICIAL: That man's death changed everything.
MOCTEZUMA PEON: Changed what?
LOW OFFICIAL: Now there's a crime.
MOCTEZUMA PEON: That has nothing to do with my men.
LOW OFFICIAL: Maybe.
MOCTEZUMA PEON: It wasn't my fault.
LOW OFFICIAL: It's your fault that violence broke out.
MOCTEZUMA PEON: If you'd let me do things my way, I could have solved everything neatly. And don't doubt it for a minute, Cantu, I'm still going to solve it.
LOW OFFICIAL: Not anymore.
MOCTEZUMA PEON: Mark my word.
LOW OFFICIAL: You seem to forget that we're all in the same boat and all fighting for the same cause.
MOCTEZUMA PEON: Do you really think so?
LOW OFFICIAL: I really think so.
MOCTEZUMA PEON: Then why don't you tell them that?
LOW OFFICIAL: Tell who?
MOCTEZUMA PEON: The guys who killed Salcido. . . They're in the same boat with us, aren't they?
LOW OFFICIAL: That's precisely what Mrs. Magaña wants to clear up. That's the crux of the matter. Let her take care of it, Mr. Moctezuma. There's no more glory, no more fame, no more money in it for you if you get in our way than if you let us take care of it. . . Explain it to your boss, he'll understand.
MOCTEZUMA PEON: *(Controlling his anger)* I can't believe how stupid you people are, Cantu!

Moctezuma Peon gets up and leaves the office.

SCENE 8

Week 2. Monday night. Between 11 and 12 p.m.
Main Action: Space 7: Taco Restaurant

Simultaneous Actions

Space 1: News room

Efren has finished his work and is beginning to put his things away while the Errand Boy is trying to convince him to sell him his tape recorder. Efren says no, emphatically. He meticulously puts his tape recorder, his paper, and his notebooks into his desk and then locks the drawer with a padlock. He leaves the News room, very tired. As soon as Efren leaves, the Errand Boy (the only person left in the News room) begins trying to open the reporter's drawer, as he will do all during the scene. At the end of the scene he achieves his goal and takes out the tape recorder. Then he locks the drawer again with the padlock.

Space 2: Apartment Building

In Dalila's apartment, Pato seems to be giving up his search. He collapses into an armchair; everything is dark.

In the Neighbor's apartment, the Neighbor is sleeping.

On the roof, the Shoeshine Boy has climbed on to the water tank and taken a large plastic bag from the inside of it. From this bag he takes another one, which contains yet another bag, etc. From the last bag he takes a bundle of bills held together by an elastic band. He adds a few more bills to the bundle and returns it to a bag, which he places within another bag, etc. He ends by hiding the largest bag in the water tank.

Space 3: Cantina

Several customers are occupying the tables. Moctezuma Peon and his Assistant are drinking at the bar. Moctezuma drinks one after another.

Space 5: Casablanca Club

Completely drunk, Waitress Antonia is sitting on the floor singing romantic songs during the whole scene.

Space 8: Gerda's House

Helped by Dalila, Gerda has arrived home. she enters alone. She turns on the light. The room is still a total mess, after the possible agents came in and turned it inside out, looking for the papers. Gerda moves furniture which is in her path and sits on a sofa. She cries quietly. She turns on the television set.

Space 9: Cabaret

At a table Low Official is drinking, accompanied by Toño, whom he has just met. He buys him a drink and they chat, very friendly.

Space 7: Taco Restaurant

Pepe and Juan Jose walk slowly down the street. They cross the street in front of the Taco Restaurant and go through the glass door. They are the only customers. They lean on the counter. They examine the taco list written on a board with movable letters.

JUAN JOSE: What are you gonna have?
PEPE: You order.
JUAN JOSE: Me... *(To the Taco Seller:)* I'll start out with four beef tacos and a beer.
PEPE: I'll take two pork and a melted cheese.
JUAN JOSE: No beer?
PEPE: No, just a soda. *(To the Taco Seller:)* A Sprite for me. Do you have Sprite?
TACO SELLER: Yeah.
PEPE: Sprite then.

The Taco Seller starts preparing the order. Pepe and Juan Jose watch him for awhile. They seem lost in thought.

Space 3: Cantina

Walking down the street, while they converse, Rosamaria and Ric cross in front of the cantina. Ric tries to make her go in.

No One Knows Anything 75

RIC: Just one drink and we'll leave, Rosy.
ROSAMARIA: No.
RIC: One drink. Real quick. . . I need to talk to you. It's serious.

Rosamaria acts surprised.

RIC: It's just that. . . I. . . *(He tries to kiss her.)*
ROSAMARIA: *(Pushing him away)* What are you doing, Ricardo?

Ricardo keeps at it. He pulls at her. He wants to embrace her and kiss her at all costs. She pushes him away.

ROSAMARIA: Let me go. Don't grab at me. I'm leaving. If you want to go in there, go ahead.

Rosamaria starts to run. Ric stands still, frustrated. Then he enters the cantina and starts drinking, at a table.

JUAN JOSE: They're sons of bitches, Pepe. Real sons of bitches.
PEPE: Why's that?
JUAN JOSE: What do you mean why? That little lawyer is a shithead and Magaña, the famous Mrs. Magaña is a disgusting old whore. *(Pause.)* They killed poor Salcido and now they don't know where their papers are.
PEPE: They didn't do it, how can you say that?
JUAN JOSE: Who, then?
PEPE: That's the problem.
JUAN JOSE: They're still sons of bitches.

Space 2: Apartment Building

After leaving Gerda in her house, Dalila returns to her apartment. She opens the door and emits a terrified scream when she sees Pato the Masseur. He tries to justify his presence, to tell her he's looking for Salcido's papers, that he's just carrying out official orders. . . Dalila doesn't let him say anymore; she throws him out. She remains alone, taciturn, seated in an armchair.

JUAN JOSE: God, those papers must be important for all this to be happening. Pepe, don't you think? I never imagined. . .
PEPE: Me neither.
JUAN JOSE: It gives me the creeps.

PEPE: Yep.
JUAN JOSE: You've got to find them, Pepe. Just think. They might give us our own Watergate... A Mexican Watergate. Not bad, huh? About time. I can see us now, just like those two gringo journalists, remember? The ones who put the screws to Nixon. Wouldn't you like to put the screws to the whole system? We could just put a scare into them this time and then later on we could go for the big time. Why not? That's how revolutions are started. *(Pause.)* What's so funny?
PEPE: The stupid things coming out of your mouth.
JUAN JOSE: Why stupid? Just 'cause I'd like to put a dent in the system?
PEPE: You can't do that in this country.
JUAN JOSE: Depends on what you're armed with. It all depends.

Silence. They drink their beer and soda which the Taco Seller has served them.

Space 9: Cabaret

Low Official and Toño have continued drinking. Low Official makes a pass at Toño, trying to caress him. Toño immediately reacts with violence. He jumps up from the table, shouting.

TOÑO: Fuckin' queer! Fuckin' queer!

A ruckus breaks out. Low Official feigns innocence. The Waiter and other customers in the cabaret remove Toño from the cabaret by pushing and shoving him. Low Official remains a while longer, drinking and looking innocent.

Pepe takes from his pocket the key Dalila sent to him. Juan Jose sees it.

JUAN JOSE: You had that all this time?

Pepe nods. He stares at the key, examines it.

PEPE: It could be a key to a suitcase, couldn't it?
JUAN JOSE: It's hard to say. We'd have to start by searching Salcido's place. You going there?

No One Knows Anything

PEPE: Yeah.

JUAN JOSE: When?

PEPE: Tomorrow. I don't think I'll find anything, but we need to look anyway.

JUAN JOSE: Be careful Pepe, will you? It could be dangerous... You want me to go with you?

Space 3: Cantina

Accompanied by his Assistant, Moctezuma Peon has continued drinking at the bar. He is by now very drunk.

MOCTEZUMA PEON: Fuckin' bitch, fuckin' bitch, fuckin' bitch. She doesn't know who she's dealin' with... She'll find out what it's like to deal with me.

The telephone rings. The Bartender picks up the receiver and gives it almost immediately to Moctezuma Peon.

BARTENDER: Telephone, boss.

Moctezuma takes the phone.

MOCTEZUMA PEON:
--Moctezuma Peon here.
--
--What?
--
--You sure?
--
--I'm on my way. Don't budge from that spot even to protect your dick.

Moctezuma, falling down drunk, goes toward the rest rooms. He urinates and then snorts some coke. He recovers slowly. He straightens his clothing, walks out.

MOCTEZUMA PEON: *(To his Assistant)* Let's go, brother. Move it.

Moctezuma Peon and his Assistant leave the Cantina rapidly. At one of the tables Ric, taciturn, is still drinking.

Pepe has been absorbed in his own thoughts for a few minutes. Maybe he and Juan Jose have started to eat the tacos they ordered from the Taco Seller. Suddenly, as if a brilliant idea had come into his head, he reacts excitedly.

PEPE: What an idiot!
JUAN JOSE: Huh?
PEPE: I'm an idiot, Johnny. . . what an idiot! You know something? I know what that fuckin' key is to.

Pepe and Juan Jose remain silent for a few minutes. Juan Jose is looking out at the street and he sees something in front of them which makes him react instinctively.

JUAN JOSE: Look at that car, Pepe. Shit!

Juan Jose has seen the danger just in time and, accompanying his words with action, throws himself to the floor, pushing his friend down too. The round of what could be machine gun fire breaks the glass door of the Taco restaurant, at the same time as the noise of a car taking off is heard. Assistants A and B from the Government Offices can be seen in the car.

Juan Jose and Pepe, on the floor, have not been hit by the machine gun fire. The Taco Seller is also safe, crouching behind the counter. A few seconds go by. Juan Jose and Pepe begin to straighten up. The Taco Seller also gets up, furious.

TACO SELLER: God-damned mother fuckers!

SCENE 9

Week 2. Tuesday morning. 7 a.m.

Main action: Space 5: Casablanca Club

Simultaneous actions

Space 1: News room

As in Scene 6, the Errand Boy has slept in the News room and, upon waking, carries out the whole ceremony of folding his blankets, putting his pad away and preparing his coffee. This time he is enjoying himself, listening to music from a cassette he is playing on the tape recorder. He is pleased with it. At the end of the scene he hides it.

Space 2: Apartment Building

Dalila is sleeping in her bedroom.

Outside the building, carrying a tiered tray of gelatins, the Neighbor is waiting for the Taco Seller. He doesn't arrive. She gets impatient. She walks to the flower stand and sees that the Florist is sad because of some family problem. She consoles her, gives her advice and gives her a religious card and some rosary beads.

Space 4: The Street

Efren crosses the street holding his son by the hand. He is taking him to school.

Gerda walks sadly, pulling her empty grocery cart. She is talking out loud, in German. She runs into the Shoeshine Boy and he walks along with her, never saying a word, until they both disappear.

Space 6: Government Offices

Only Low Official's Office is lit up.

In it we see the Taco Seller, alone, sunk into an armchair. Assistants A and B enter and leave the office carrying papers, but they don't stop to talk to the Taco Seller.

Space 5: Casablanca Club.

Several members are present, either on the massage table, undressing to go into the steam room or doing calisthenics. Pepe is in front of the row of lockers. Nervous, with a clandestine air, he tries to put a key in the door of one of the compartments. While he is doing this he is surprised by Pato the Masseur, who comes up to him suddenly. Pepe pretends he was doing something else.

PATO THE MASSEUR: Can I help you?
PEPE: Oh, hello.
PATO THE MASSEUR: Can I help you?
PEPE: Don't you remember me?
PATO: Of course.
PEPE: *(After a pause)* Did the agents come back to bother you? They interrogated me all day, and then. . . *(Interrupting himself:)* Luckily. . . *(Interrupting himself:)* I can't believe no one saw anything. Right here under our noses. . .

Silence.

PEPE: You knew Salcido pretty well, didn't you?

Pato nods "yes."

PEPE: He was a member here. . . for a long time, wasn't he?
PATO: At the Attorney General's Office I already said all I have to say.
PEPE: I'm not a cop. And I'm not questioning you. *(Pause.)* Salcido told you about me, didn't he?
PATO: No.
PEPE: You don't remember?

Pato shakes his head "no."

PEPE: That morning you knew I was coming. You were waiting for me. Salcido. . . *(He stops.)*

Silence.

PATO: What were you looking for?

PEPE: Me?
PATO: In the lockers.
PEPE: I came to look for you. I wanted to talk to you about a few things, but it looks like you don't trust me.
PATO: In the lockers.
PEPE: What?
PATO: You were trying to open them.

Space 6: Government Offices

As he comes and goes to and from Low Official's Office, Assistant A finally stops in front of the Taco Seller.

ASSISTANT A: Where were we, Popeye? *(Transition. Looking at a page from a file.)* You are Popeye, aren't you? Popeye Dominguez, native of Coatzacoalcos, Veracruz, sailor during the seventies... Where were we?
TACO SELLER: You were talking about some dough, sir, to fix up my place.
ASSISTANT A: First we have to clear this thing up, Popeye... With all the problems you have with everybody and his uncle, I can't just go defending you for no reason.
TACO SELLER: I don't have problems with nobody, sir.
ASSISTANT: We'll see if that's true or not. *(Pause.)* Just a minute.

Assistant A leaves the office again and the Taco Seller is alone. From now until the end of the scene, the same action is repeated: Assistants A and B entering and leaving.

PEPE: I was looking for Salcido's locker. He said he would leave something in it for me.
PATO: That's a lie.
PEPE: No, it's true. Really.
PATO: No.
PEPE: He even gave me the key.
PATO: He didn't have a key. I keep them all. *(Pause.)* Allow me...
PEPE: What?
PATO: Let me see the key you say Lorenzo gave you... To show you it doesn't fit.

Silence. Pepe is hesitant about showing him the key. Pato takes from his pocket a key chain full of small locker keys. Pepe makes up his mind and takes his out. He compares it with Pato's.

PATO: Not at all alike. Not even close.

Pepe realizes they're different.

PATO: That's from somewhere else.
PEPE: Yeah.
PATO: What was Salcido supposed to leave you in his locker?
PEPE: Just a favor... Doesn't make any difference now.
PATO: Well he didn't leave anything... The day of the accident, the first thing the cops did was look for all of Salcido's things. I opened up the locker myself.

Pato the Masseur signals for Pepe to follow him and he takes a few steps forward. They stop in front of one of the lockers.

PATO: This was his... And here's the key. *(He opens the locker. It is empty.)* There wasn't anything in it. Nothing interesting anyway... His tennis shoes, his lotions, his underwear... They took everything. They were supposed to give it all to the family later. That's what they said, anyway, but you know how that goes. *(Pause.)* There wasn't anything that could've been for you. No papers.
PEPE: And would you happen to know... *(He stops.)*
PATO: No, I don't know anything.

Silence. Pepe prepares to leave, defeated.

PEPE: Oh, well.
PATO: We're real sorry about Salcido's accident. All of us here are real sorry. We liked him.
PEPE: Yeah.
PATO: *(suddenly emphatic)* That key's not from here, I can guarantee you. Not from any part of the gym.
PEPE: Thanks.

Pepe turns around to leave. Pato stops him.

PATO: Why don't you speak with Mrs. Gerda? Lorenzo's mother... Maybe she can help you find what you're looking for.
PEPE: Thanks.

Pepe leaves. Pato goes to the table, where a club member is lying, face down. Pato begins the massage. The man raises his head for a moment to speak.

MEMBER: That kid's gonna end up with a bullet in his head.
PATO: Yep.

SCENE 10

Week 2. Between 9 and 10 p.m.

Main Action: Space 8: Gerda's House

Simultaneous actions

Space 1: News room

The reporters are working. Pepe, Ric and Efren are absent. Shoeshine Boy shines Errand Boy's shoes. Rosamaria is explaining to Juan Jose that Managing Editor Sagrario is very upset with him. Then Sagrario arrives, accompanied by Efren, and goes into her private office. Efren has discovered by now the theft of his tape recorder and he approaches the Errand Boy about it, but the latter feigns innocence. Efren sits down at his desk to work.

Space 2: Apartment Building

The Neighbor is suffering from an anxiety attack provoked by her insomnia. During the entire scene she paces from one side to another, taking pills and apparently getting angry with the image of the Sacred Heart. She takes the flowers she had put in a vase in honor of the image and throws them into the street. Then she turns the image around and takes from the lower extreme of it a bottle of liquor she had hidden there. She begins to drink. While the Neighbor drinks, near the end of the scene, see Assistants A and B breaking into the building. They climb onto the roof.

Space 3: Cantina

The Bartender is very busy because Waitress Antonia is not there. Toño has returned to the Cantina. He is sitting at a table. He is drinking but he is also writing prolifically.

Space 5: The Casablanca Club

Pato the Masseur is alone, in his area, preparing his lotions. Quite a bit into the scene he gets frightened because he hears footsteps and noises of people approaching. He turns off the lights and hides.

Space 6: Government Offices

Low Official, in his office, is talking very cordially with Ric. Ric has shown him some pages and photos of what could be an article, and Low Official looks them over, satisfied. They both look very satisfied.

Space 7: Taco Restaurant

While Agent 2 makes a phone call in a booth near the Taco Restaurant, Agent 1 eats an order of tacos. The Taco Seller turns away for a moment and Agent 1 furtively tries to steal the money that the Taco Seller has put into the drawer. The Taco Seller sees Agent 1 just in time and he drives his knife into the counter, very near where Agent 1's hand was creeping along. Agent 1 smiles as if it were all a game, but the Taco Seller maintains his fierce stance. When Agent 2 finishes his phone call, both agents depart.

Space 9: Cabaret

Lots of activity in the Cabaret. Waitress Antonia and the Florist converse for a few minutes. Waitress Antonia confesses to her friend that she is very in love with Toño. The Florist tries to talk her out of her sentiment, but Waitress Antonia reaffirms her feelings. At the end of the scene she leaves to look for Toño, heading for the Cantina.

Space 8: Gerda's House

Gerda is sitting in front of her television set, which is on; she is punching buttons on her remote control channel changer, running continuously through the channels, at times impulsively. She never seems satisfied with the program she has chosen and keeps searching for others. Her feverish television activity doesn't keep her from talking coherently and following the thread of her conversation or her monologues, at the same time comprehending what is being projected on to the screen. She is talking to Pepe, who is seated near her, also facing the television set. At a distance, in a corner of the room, also facing the set, is Dalila, absorbed in her knitting. The room they are in still shows signs of the destruction caused by the agents shortly after the death of Salcido. Gerda hasn't finished cleaning the place up.

GERDA: My God, these programs are terrible, just terrible. *(She changes channels several times. Transition.)* Then the children's father died and I was alone with them. It was especially hard because of Dalila's problem. There wasn't any cure. I spent all the money I had, for nothing. I went back to Rostock for a while, with my family, and then we went to London, to that hospital in Romania, and to Houston. I don't know where else to go.

Space 6: Government Offices

*High Official bursts into Low Official's office, where the latter is conversing with Ric. She throws the afternoon newspapers--*Ovaciones *and* La Extra*-- on to his desk, in the faces of Low Official and Ric.*

HIGH OFFICIAL: If I go under, you two go under!... What do you have to say about this, Cantu? Haven't you seen them? Haven't you read either *Ovaciones* or *La Extra*?
RIC: Those aren't my papers.
HIGH OFFICIAL: *(To Low Official)* You led me to believe everything was under control, and look at this.
LOW OFFICIAL: Everything *is* under control.
HIGH OFFICIAL: Then how do you explain this?

LOW OFFICIAL: What?
HIGH OFFICIAL: Can't you read?. . . They want me to testify. The deputies want me to testify in the Chamber.
LOW OFFICIAL: You know as well as I do the opposition will do anything. . .
HIGH OFFICIAL: No, Cantu. . . It wasn't the opposition. My testimony was requested by our colleagues in the PRI!

High Official goes into her office, slamming the door. Low Official and Ric look at each other with surprise. From this moment on, during the whole scene, High Official will be talking on the phone and ordering Low Official about. The latter will go in and out of his boss' office, place calls for her, take files to her, etc., aided at times by Ric.

GERDA: Where else did we take you, Dalila, what other hospitals?
DALILA: Havana.
GERDA: Oh, yes, of course, Havana, too, for all that was worth. No place we took her could find a way to cure her because her problem wasn't in her body, it was in her imagination, beyond fantasy, you might say. *(Changing the channels.)* They even wanted to put her in an insane asylum but there wasn't any point either in an asylum or a mental hospital, since there wasn't any cure. There's no way to help her find her way or to help her at all, because the help that a delicate soul needs in these circumstances, in cases like hers, like my dear, dear daughter's *(changing the channel)*; the help she really needs, mister, is just to be taken care of. She needs to be spoiled, to be petted. That's what my dear departed Chano used to say, may he rest in peace, my beloved son, look how he ended up in this terrible tragedy. *(Changes the channels several times. Long pause.)* He used to protect her when I couldn't protect her anymore because my strength and my patience were all used up. Especially my patience. At my age, I just couldn't deal with it anymore. I couldn't stand my poor Dalila anymore. Right, Dalila? Isn't it true I couldn't stand you anymore? I even considered, once, taking her to that asylum I was talking about. We went to see it. It wasn't close. South of the city. Beyond Tlalpan, I think, maybe Contreras. That's it, Contreras. The building was huge, very well kept, with a nice yard, all kinds of games; I think it even had a swimming pool. She liked it a lot and so did I, but not enough to leave her there. Chano said absolutely not. Chano said no. So he

took her somewhere else so I wouldn't have to deal with her because I simply couldn't. *(Changes channels.)* My health was failing. My poor deteriorated health. . . He took her from my side. Chano. . . always so good to me. He took her to Guadalajara to live so I wouldn't be burdened.

Space 1: News room

Summoned by Managing Editor Sagrario, Juan Jose has gone into her office. The Editor is talking to him.

EDITOR: What happened to your interview with Fidel?
JUAN JOSE: I ran into some problems.
EDITOR: With the CTM's press agent?
JUAN JOSE: Personal problems, ma'am.

EDITOR: *(Interrupting)* No excuses, Juan Jose. . . I won't take one more excuse. Do what you're told, and then we'll talk. And if you don't like it, you know what you can do. The door is open. You can return to the *Excelsior*, to work with Regino. You used to love working with him, didn't you?

Editor Sagrario makes a gesture and Juan Jose gets up and returns to the News room. He goes back to work. Later Efren goes into the Editor's office and speaks privately with her.

GERDA: He had you there a long time, didn't he, Dalila? Do you remember when Chano took you to Guadalajara to live?
DALILA: We were very happy in Guadalajara.
GERDA: But then they had to come back because Chano had a lot to do here and he couldn't just leave everything to take care of his poor sick sister. He came back and before long he rented an apartment for her, in the San Rafael district, I think. You've been there, I think, haven't you? A simple apartment, but fine for her, for her illness. Very nice. *(Changes the channel several times.)* That's where she spends all her days and nights writing her poems. Beautiful poems, very pretty. Mysterious, of course, since they're coming out of a mind that flies, flies, flies through the fantasies of consciousness. She writes them but she signs them with another name. Hasn't she recited any of them for you?. . . Has she recited them for you yet? Has she recited them?

PEPE: Well, yes, a few of them. . .
GERDA: And she uses a pseudonym. She invented a name for herself so she could say that those poems aren't by her but by another person named Concha Urquiza. *(She changes the channel several times.)*

Space 5: Casablanca Club
Moctezuma Peon and his Assistant have finally entered the club and they find Pato the Masseur, who is hiding, trembling. Moctezuma Peon's Assistant beats him and then, with Pato's own tie, tries to strangle him, helped by the Assistant.

MOCTEZUMA PEON: What's the key to?
PATO: I don't know.
MOCTEZUMA PEON: What do you mean, you don't know?
PATO: I don't know.
MOCTEZUMA PEON: You're about to remember.
PATO: *(Giving up)* It could be his sister's.
MOCTEZUMA PEON: Whose sister's?
PATO: His sister's.
MOCTEZUMA PEON: Salcido's sister? Salcido had a sister?
PATO: Yes.
MOCTEZUMA PEON: Where does she live?
PATO: I don't know.
MOCTEZUMA PEON: Where does she live, you motherfucker!
PATO: Serapio Rendon.
MOCTEZUMA PEON: What number?
PATO: I don't remember.
MOCTEZUMA PEON: What number?!!
PATO: One twenty four, I think.
MOCTEZUMA PEON: You think or you're sure?
PATO: I'm sure.
MOCTEZUMA PEON: Say it again.
PATO: Say what?
MOCTEZUMA PEON: The address.
PATO: One twenty four Serapio Rendon.

They release him.

MOCTEZUMA PEON: See? See how easy it is to tell the truth? *(Pause.)* Poor thing, he's sweating.

> *Moctezuma Peon's Assistant drags Pato the Masseur to the shower area. They put him, fully dressed, under one of the showers and turn it on. The stream of water falls on him for a good while. He remains lying there, semi-conscious, as Moctezuma and his Assistant leave the place.*

GERDA: Now that my dearest Chano has died, I don't know what I'm going to do with Dalila. *(Transition.)* What am I going to do with you, Dalila? Eh? What will I do? Tell me, will you?
DALILA: You don't have to do anything, mother.
GERDA: I can't take care of you. Not by myself, I can't. . . Maybe you, since you were a friend of Chano's, maybe you could help me. Couldn't you? *(Transition)* TV is so bad. Terrible! *(Changes channels.)* See what happens to a man who wants to fight for truth? They kill him. . . You saw. They killed him. I told Chano plenty of times, didn't I, Dalila? We both told him. If you keep messing with those guys they're going to kill you. . . In this country you can't fight for justice, nor truth nor for what's right, because you'll end up like that, like he ended up: running away, hiding, dead. . . But why am I telling you all this? You were his friend, you know more than I do. *(Changes channels.)* He never used to tell me anything about what he was involved with. . . He wanted to protect me, he used to say, and that's why he wouldn't tell me. Now they come to interrogate me and turn the house inside out. . . you should have seen how they tore this place apart! They barged in, broke everything, turned everything on its head! It was awful, those were two awful days. *(Changes channels.)*
PEPE: You say they came to search the house?
GERDA: That's right. Four officers from the judicial police, is what they said. How would I know? And they destroyed almost everything. Just take a look, if you want. You can see how they left the rooms. I haven't picked anything up. Dalila helped me a little, but not much.
PEPE: They made a real mess.
GERDA: That's right, a real mess. Isn't that right, Dalila? *(Changes channels.)*
PEPE: What were they looking for?
GERDA: I don't know. I don't have any idea.
PEPE: An important document, maybe.
GERDA: You can be sure about that. . . But they didn't find it. *(Changing the channel).* They looked everywhere for it, but

they didn't find it. *(Smiling).* No way there were going to find it. My Chano was nobody's fool.
PEPE: Did they miss any place?
GERDA: What do you mean?
PEPE: Is there any place they didn't look?
GERDA: What do you think? They looked everywhere. They turned everything upside down, to the last corner of the kitchen.
PEPE: Did they look in the suitcases?
GERDA: What suitcases?
PEPE: In your son's suitcases. *(Pause.)* I imagine your son had suitcases.
GERDA: Oh, yes. He used to travel a lot.
PEPE: And he had suitcases.
GERDA: Of course. He had some black leather suitcases, very pretty. Really beautiful, weren't they, Dalila? *(Changes channels.)*
PEPE: They must have looked through those suitcases, too. . . the agents.

For the first time, Gerda seems to be interested in what she sees on the television set. She concentrates and calls Pepe's attention.

GERDA: Look, look.

Pause. Gerda stares at the television screen. She turns to Pepe again.

GERDA: I'm sorry. You were saying. . .?
PEPE: I was asking you if the policemen, those officers who came to mess up your house, if they also looked in your son's suitcases.
GERDA: Well, I really don't know. I guess they did. I haven't looked at them.
PEPE: Could we check?
GERDA: Of course. *(Pause.)* Why? *(Changes the channel.)*

Pepe takes the key from his pocket and dangles it in front of Gerda.

PEPE: I think this key, which your son gave me, goes to one of those suitcases.
GERDA: What key?

In response, Pepe makes the presence of the key more obvious. Gerda leans forward and looks at it more closely. She smiles.

GERDA: That key isn't from any suitcase. That's from Dalila's desk. Right, Dalila?

Dalila doesn't respond. She pretends to be absorbed in her knitting. Gerda changes channels a few times. Pepe is visibly disconcerted.

GERDA: Unmistakable. . . A beautiful secretaire we brought from Germany, my deceased husband and I. From Austria. A family piece. . . later Chano took it to Dalila to her apartment, right, Dalila?
PEPE: Are you sure?
GERDA: Of course I'm sure.
PEPE: The key goes to that desk?
GERDA: Unmistakable. It's a family jewel, I'm telling you.

Pepe turns to Dalila, who has suspended her knitting.

PEPE: Did you know that?

Dalila nods her head "yes."

PEPE: *(Disconcerted)* But you're the one who gave it to me. . . *(He stops.)* Why didn't you tell me that the key/
DALILA: You didn't ask me, love.

While Gerda changes the channel, Pepe gets up suddenly, grabs Dalila by the wrist and pulls her to her feet. Her knitting falls to the floor. Pepe pulls her toward the door, as if he were suddenly in a great hurry. Gerda stops Pepe by calling out to him.

GERDA: Excuse me, sir. . .

Pepe turns to her.

GERDA: Take care of her. She's the only thing. . . the last thing I have left in this world.

Pepe and Dalila leave. Gerda stares at the screen. She changes channels compulsively.

SCENE 11

Week 2. Tuesday night. Between 10 and 11 p.m.

Main Action: Space 2: Apartment Building

Simultaneous Actions

Space 1:   News room

The journalistic activity begun in the previous scene continues. Juan Jose, in a very bad mood because of the scolding from the Managing Editor, is writing. Rosamaria is with the Errand Boy and is nervous because the photocopier is not working. Efren is talking with the Editor in her private office. He later leaves and calls to Rosamaria to tell her the Editor wants to talk to her. Rosamaria enters the private office. Meanwhile, in a corner of the News room, Shoeshine Boy is cleaning up a pile of women's shoes, most probably belonging to the Managing Editor.

Space 3:   Cantina

Waitress Antonia has finally reached the Cantina and is at a table talking to Toño. The latter has stopped writing and is clearly drunk again. The Bartender is unhappy because Waitress Antonia is talking to Toño rather than doing her work.

Space 6:   Government Offices

High Official and Low Official are talking with Ric, in the main office, probably about the article Ric showed Low Official earlier. They interrupt their talk to watch the news on television, but they discover that the set is out of order. Ric obligingly offers to fix it and finally does. While Ric is working on the set, a telephone call causes High Official to ask Low Official and Ric to go somewhere. else They leave the office. High Official stays behind watching the news on the television.

Space 7: Taco Restaurant

A beggar enters the taco restaurant and wants to stay to eat. The Taco Seller tries to remove him but the Beggar insists on staying. From his bag he pulls out a bundle of bills and pays in advance. The Taco Seller is obliged to serve him. Later, the Beggar takes a tape recorder from the same bag, turns it on and starts to sing a ranchera song which is on the tape.

Space 8: Gerda's House

Gerda watches television while she eats a light supper. She is watching the same newscast as the one showing on High Official's set.

Space 9: Cabaret

Great activity in the cabaret. The Florist can be seen dancing with a customer.

Space 2: Apartment Building

In the Neighbor's Apartment, the Neighbor is now totally drunk. Assistants A and B maraud around on the roof of the building, looking for Dalila's apartment. They enter the Neighbor's apartment by mistake.

Pepe and Dalila arrive at the building. Pepe climbs the stairs two by two. Dalila follows him, moving slowly and deliberately, declaiming:

DALILA:

> How did I lose, through sterile chance
> the warm and mature image
> that nature gave me of itself
> implicated in your voice and your embrace.
>
> Not even the whisper of your steps,
> nor anything within your heart can last;
> you have become "maybe" in my darkness
> and emptied your being into my arms.

Pepe hurries Dalila with a gesture, but she maintains her slow rhythm. Pepe reaches the door of Apartment 5. He applies pressure with his hands trying the open the door. He is not successful.

DALILA:

>Universe without cardinal points.
>The black wind of genesis supplants
>that blonde waving of the wheat fields.

PEPE: *(Hurrying Dalila)* Come on. *(Referring to the door.)* It's really closed now.

Dalila stands immobile in front of the door, prepared to finish her poem first.

DALILA:

>And a whirlwind of shadow rises up
>there where your swift angels
>rested perhaps their serene feet.

Long silence. Pepe controls his urgency. Dalila smiles while Pepe indicates by a gesture that she should open the door.

DALILA: Are we going to make love? *(Pause.)* Answer me first.
PEPE: What do you want me to answer?
DALILA: If we're going to make love. *(Pause.)* If you say no, we're not going in.
PEPE: We're going to make love.

Dalila embraces Pepe and kisses him repeatedly on the face.

Space 1: News room
Efren and Juan Jose are working at their respective desks. The Errand Boy continues trouble-shooting with the photocopier, while the Shoeshine Boy cleans the pile of shoes. The Managing Editor is in her private office, talking to Rosamaria.

ROSAMARIA: He's been sort of hostile toward me.
EDITOR: Toward you and everyone else. What's the matter with him? Pepe's not like that.

> ROSAMARIA: He's been working too hard. I guess that's the reason.
> EDITOR: What's he working on? He finished his reports on the city and I haven't given him any new assignments. Neither has Calvo. What's he doing?

Dalila opens the apartment. They enter total darkness.

PEPE: Turn on the lights.
DALILA: The bulb's out. *(She walks through the darkness toward a little table).* But the radio's fine. *(She turns on the radio. Soft music comes out; she regulates the volume.)* So's the little lamp. *(She turns on the little table lamp that barely lights the room up.)*

Pepe has gone toward the secretaire. He puts the key in the lock and opens the desk with emotion and nervousness. It is practically empty. The only thing there is a thick spiral notebook.

PEPE: Here it is. It's been here all this time, from the beginning. . . And you knew it.

Dalila smiles and starts to undress, while she declaims. She acts out a strange, slow strip-tease, to the sound of the music and her own recitation. Pepe, in the meantime, takes the notebook, carries it to the little table and begins to read the document carefully.

DALILA:

> I want to be with you in the sacred
> silence of the night, and in your protection
> spread the wings of mortal care.
>
> Like a lover on the breast of her beloved,
> drinking her desire at length,
> I want to rejoice in solitude with you.
>
> On dark nights I guard your presence,
> and my heart blindly adores you so much
> that I possess you in luminous shadow.
>
> Without seeing you I will love you,
> if I don't, at the hour when life's dream ends,

awaken from your presence with the dawn.

But now the evening of the vanquished arrives,
and time is light and the space is brief
to keep the lamp lit.

When you give in to my warm embrace,
speak to me, sweet love, of the moment
when you are to wrap me in the eternal gown.

I will not treasure the miserable suffering
of my senses that moan, prisoners,
of the body which is fading and withering.

Nor will I hold in esteem the final word
nor the horror of the deep grave
nor the moaning of the sorrowful relatives.

Nor the vague goodness and the fleeting sweetness
that the moribund heart wakes
to the desire of life and fortune.

Because behind the uncertain parting,
beyond the pale frontier,
love watches and hope hits the mark.

There I will find you one final time,
and on your breast which has flowered from many loves
I will know eternal spring.

Before Dalila finishes reciting, almost naked by now, Pepe finishes reading. He looks anxious, impressed by something. He interrupts her.

PEPE: Dalila...
DALILA: *(Stops reciting)* Yes?
PEPE: Do you know how much this is worth? *(Pause)* Eighty thousand dollars... Eighty thousand dollars.
DALILA: Chano didn't care about the money. He just wanted a little justice, some truth... He wanted to pull off a few masks...

No One Knows Anything

Dalila stops talking. She has heard noises outside of the apartment. She is startled.

The noises are being made by Assistants A and B, in the Neighbor's apartment. They have gone into her dwelling. Drunk and very frightened, the Neighbor attacks them, as if to defend herself, and they beat her violently, finally leaving her stretched out unconscious, maybe dead. Assistants A and B are disconcerted. They realize they are in the wrong place and leave the building running.

During the noise, Dalila turns to Pepe.

DALILA: They're in there.
PEPE: Who?
DALILA: Quick, Pepe, get out of here. It's them.
PEPE: Who?
DALILA: The guys who were looking for Chano. *(Very anxious.)* Hurry up. Go.

Pepe goes toward the door. Dalila stops him.

DALILA: No. Not that way.
PEPE: Is there another door?
DALILA: *(Shakes her head "NO")* The window...

With the folder in his hands, Pepe goes toward the window. He hesitates a few minutes, thinking about Dalila.

PEPE: And you?
DALILA: They want the papers.
PEPE: I can't just leave you like this.
DALILA: I'll be fine.

A few seconds after the departure of Assistants A and B Moctezuma Peon and his Assistant have arrived at the building. Their paths almost cross. They go directly to Dalila's apartment while Pepe climbs out of the window and, grabbing on to the window sills, slides along, looking for the sidewalk. When Pepe has disappeared from view, Moctezuma Peon and his Assistant start beating down the door.

MOCTEZUMA PEON: Open up! Federal Security, open up!

Dalila has covered her nakedness with a blanket, but she remains still. Moctezuma Peon's Assistant pushes the door until it gives way. The two men burst in.

MOCTEZUMA PEON: Where's Gutierrez?
DALILA: There's no one here.

Moctezuma Peon slaps Dalila.

MOCTEZUMA PEON: We followed the two of you here, stupid. Where is he?
DALILA: *(Whining)* No. . .

Moctezuma Peon's Assistant has gone into the other rooms of the apartment and now returns. He sees the open window, the moving window shade.

PEON'S ASSISTANT: The window, boss.
MOCTEZUMA PEON: Step on it. . . Catch him!

Moctezuma Peon's Assistant leaves the apartment and starts running.

MOCTEZUMA PEON: *(To Dalila)* That was Gutierrez, right? . . Answer me, bitch!
DALILA: No. . .

He hits her in the face. She runs into the bedroom but he chases her, closes in on her and hits her again until she is on the floor, defeated. He exults cruelly in his victory. She moans.

Space 3: Cantina

The discussion between Toño and Waitress Antonia has reached a crisis point. The customers have left the restaurant. Waitress Antonia makes movements to leave. Toño holds her back.

ANTONIA: Let go of me!
TOÑO: You're not going anywhere. You stay here!
BARTENDER: *(Intervening)* Let her go, can't you hear?

No One Knows Anything

TOÑO: Nobody's talking to you, asshole. Don't mess with me or I'll bust your balls.
BARTENDER: Yeah, sure, I'll bet. You and who else, buddy? Come on, let's see you!
ANTONIA: Let's go, Toño... That's enough, please.
TOÑO: *(As he leaves, to the Bartender)* I'm gonna burn this fuckin' place down, just you wait.
BARTENDER: You good-for-nothing moocher. You little pimp!

Antonia and Toño disappear. The Bartender closes his restaurant by lowering the metal curtain.

MOCTEZUMA PEON: Get up.

Dalila moans.

MOCTEZUMA PEON: Get up, bitch, or you'll get more.

Dalila straightens up with difficulty. She is bleeding from the mouth and tries to cover her body, but Moctezuma Peon prevents her from doing so, pushing her. Dalila uses an armchair to protect herself. From there, squatting on the floor, she looks at Moctezuma Peon with terror.

MOCTEZUMA PEON: Now you're going to tell me everything I want to know... That man who was with you, who jumped from the window... it was Gutierrez, wasn't it? The journalist.

Dalila nods.

MOCTEZUMA PEON: Did he have the papers with him?
DALILA: I don't know.
MOCTEZUMA PEON: Did he have the papers your brother stole or not, bitch? Answer!
DALILA: No.
MOCTEZUMA PEON: I want the truth, bitch!

Moctezuma Peon begins to beat Dalila again. She tries to stop his hands. She is whining.

DALILA: No more, no more, no more...
MOCTEZUMA PEON: Then answer! Did he have the papers?
DALILA: Yes.
MOCTEZUMA PEON: The papers your brother stole.
DALILA: Yes.
MOCTEZUMA PEON: Are you sure?
DALILA: Yes.

Moctezuma Peon's Assistant returns to the apartment. He is panting.

PEON'S ASSISTANT: I didn't catch him, boss.
MOCTEZUMA PEON: You idiot.
PEON'S ASSISTANT: He got away. He had a head start... Looks like he grabbed a taxi.
MOCTEZUMA PEON: Did you see him?
PEON'S ASSISTANT: I'm not sure, but I think so. He was way ahead of me.
MOCTEZUMA PEON: We can still catch him at the newspaper. I'm sure...

Moctezuma Peon stops and becomes pensive. He goes to the phone. Moctezuma Peon's Assistant stops forward, solicitous.

PEON'S ASSISTANT: Want me to place the call, boss?
MOCTEZUMA PEON: *(Changing his mind)* No, not from this phone. *(Pause.)* I'm going to leave you here, taking care of this little dear.
PEON'S ASSISTANT: Me?
MOCTEZUMA PEON: You're gonna answer for her with your life, you bastard.
PEON'S ASSISTANT: Whatever you say, boss.
MOCTEZUMA PEON: I won't be long.

Moctezuma Peon's Assistant stops his boss before he leaves.

PEON'S ASSISTANT: While you're gone, can I fool around with her? *(He smiles.)*
MOCTEZUMA PEON: Just don't hurt her.
MOCTEZUMA PEON: Thanks, boss.

Moctezuma Peon leaves the apartment.

> **Space 6: Government Offices**
>
> While she watches the news on television, High Official hears the network phone ring. She springs up from her seat, picks up the receiver and listens a long time without speaking.
>
> **HIGH OFFICIAL**: *(Into the phone, emphatically)* I guarantee you, those papers will be returned to where they belong.

SCENE 12

Week 2. Tuesday night. Between 11 and 11:30 p.m.

Main action: Space 1: News room.

> **Simultaneous actions**
>
> **Space 2: Apartment building**
>
> *Moctezuma Peon's Assistant is alone, facing Dalila.*
>
> *First he pretends to treat her with kindness and tenderness, but he ends up abusing her brutally. Dalila doesn't resist the sexual attack.*
>
> **Space 3: Cantina**
>
> *With the metal curtain of his establishment lowered, the Bartender sweeps and cleans the inside of the Cantina.*
>
> **Space 6: Government Offices**
>
> *High Official continues to watch the television news. From time to time she makes a telephone call.*
>
> **Space 7: Taco Restaurant**
>
> *The Beggar with the appearance of the garbage picker finishes eating and leaves. The Taco Seller waits on new customers.*

> **Space 8: Gerda's House**
>
> Gerda continues to watch television. At the end of the scene, there is a knock at the door and she goes to open it. It is Pato the Masseur, all beat up after Moctezuma Peon's attack in the steam room. Pato falls, unconscious, at Gerda's feet.
>
> **Space 9: Cabaret**
>
> The animated activity continues.

Space 1: News room

Efren is at his desk, writing. The Shoeshine Boy is still in the corner shining the pile of shoes. In front of the photocopy machine, which is out of order, are Rosamaria and Juan Jose. Rosamaria is upset because the machine is stuck. Juan Jose is helping her.

ROSAMARIA: *(To Juan Jose)* Don't touch it. Listen to me. It's dangerous.
ERRAND BOY: *(Coming from the Editor's office)* She needs those copies right now. She's asking for them. She says now. She's all pissed off.
ROSAMARIA: And what can I do if the stupid Xerox machine won't work.
JUAN JOSE: *(To the Errand Boy)* Go get Piolin.
ERRAND BOY: Piolin doesn't hang around here this time of night.
EFREN: *(From his place)* Camarena knows how to fix it. He went up to the third floor... Go get him, Gofer.
JUAN JOSE: And hurry.
ERRAND BOY: Why me, everything me, me, me. I can't go.

Errand Boy leaves and returns several times. He stumbles.

ROSAMARIA: I'll try to get Camarena on the phone... *(Dials a number.)*
--Chabelita?
--Chabelita, do me a favor. Can you find Camarena around there? The Xerox machine is stuck.

Ric enters the News room, followed by Low Official.

ROSAMARIA: *(Into the phone)* Thanks. *(She hangs up.)*
RIC: *(To Rosamaria)* This gentleman is here to talk to Sagrario.
ROSAMARIA: Mr. . .
RIC: Mr. Joaquin Cantu.
ROSAMARIA: *(Reacting)* Oh, yes, excuse me, sir. Mrs. Sagrario is expecting you. This way, please.
LOW OFFICIAL: Thank you, don't get up.
ROSAMARIA: It's no trouble, sir.

As Rosamaria approaches to accompany Low Official to the Managing Editor's private office, she turns to Ric.

ROSAMARIA: Juanito Miranda is waiting for you in the lab, with the photographs for the supplement. He says they're ready.
RIC: *(Suddenly remembering)* Oh, God, that's right. *(He hurries toward another area. He says to Low Official as he leaves:)* I'll see you shortly, sir. Excuse me.
LOW OFFICIAL: Of course, Ricardo, go on.

Ric leaves quickly. Low Official stops briefly in front of Juan Jose's desk. Juan Jose gets up.

LOW OFFICIAL: Good evening, Mr. Tagle. What a pleasure to see you.
JUAN JOSE: Good evening.
LOW OFFICIAL: And your friend Gutierrez? I don't see him.
JUAN JOSE: He's not here yet. He's on the street. . . hunting down juicy political news.
LOW OFFICIAL: This time of night?
JUAN JOSE: That's right.
LOW OFFICIAL: Give him my regards when he gets here. Unless I see him first.
JUAN JOSE: Sure thing.

Low Official walks toward the Editor's office. He and Rosamaria disappear into the office.

Space 4: The Street

Toño and Waitress Antonia walk down the street. They stop to quarrel.

TOÑO: You're gonna do it for me now. For me and nobody else.
ANTONIA: But when it comes time you can't even get it up...
TOÑO: Hey...
ANTONIA: You're always drunk.
TOÑO: You'll see how drunk I am.

Toño throws himself on Waitress Antonia. They struggle.

ANTONIA: Get away. You're disgusting. Get away.

Antonia hits Toño. They fall to the ground. Antonia gets up.

ANTONIA: I've had enough, you bastard. This time I've really had enough.
TOÑO: *(Stretched out on the ground)* No, Toña, no... Don't go, Antonia!... Antonia!

Antonia disappears down the street. Toño runs after her.

Camarena the Mechanic enters the News room and starts to fix the photocopy machine. After awhile Pepe arrives, panting. He goes to Juan Jose, near the receptionist. They both try to look as casual as possible, but Efren notices the mysterious air about them. He pretends not to notice them.

JUAN JOSE: *(Upon seeing Pepe)* Hey, look, I was just...
PEPE: *(Interrupting him, showing him the folder)* Keep a lookout.
JUAN JOSE: Don't tell me you got the papers...
PEPE: Figure out a way to steal a look at them.
JUAN JOSE: Salcido's papers?

Juan Jose opens the folder and tries to get a quick idea of its contents. Pepe doesn't let him; he takes it from him. From a distance, Efren and the Shoeshine Boy, separately, keep their eyes on the two reporters.

PEPE: Later.
JUAN JOSE: *(Interested in the folder)* Wait a minute.
PEPE: There's deep shit, Juan Jose. Dalila's trapped in her apartment with the guys who're looking for this.
JUAN JOSE: *(Looking at the papers)* God Almighty! Did you see this?

PEPE: I need your help.
JUAN JOSE: *(Same)* This is dynamite. We're gonna have to find a paper that'll have the guts to publish this. *(Transition.)* No. Better yet: The Chamber of Deputies. We'll go to the Deputies from the opposition party and let them take care of it... I think this time you've got the story of the year, pal.
PEPE: First we have to do something to help that girl.
JUAN JOSE: *(Distracted, thinking about the documents)* What?
PEPE: You've got to help me.
JUAN JOSE: *(About the documents)* Now I see why they're about to shit their pants. You know who's here, with Sagrario? Cantu. He asked about you.
PEPE: First you have to help me with Dalila.
JUAN JOSE: Dalila?
PEPE: Salcido's sister. She got me the documents.
JUAN JOSE: *(Finally getting interested)* What about her?
PEPE: She's with those guys. I got away.
JUAN JOSE: First the document. Too bad the Xerox machine... *(To the Errand Boy, who is going by right then.)* Did the machine get fixed?
ERRAND BOY: The rollers are shot. Camarena says it'll be tomorrow. He's got to get the part.

Rosamaria returns from the Editor's private office. She sees Pepe and she goes quickly to him.

ROSAMARIA: Sagrario's been asking about you. She wants to see you. It's urgent.
PEPE: No way.
JUAN JOSE: *(To Rosamaria)* Guess what this is?

A phone rings. Rosamaria picks it up immediately.

ROSAMARIA: *(To Juan Jose)* No kidding?
JUAN JOSE: No kidding.

Simultaneous scenes

The person calling the News room, from a public phone booth, is Moctezuma Peon.

ROSAMARIA: *(Into the phone)* Good evening. News room.

MOCTEZUMA PEON: *(Into the phone)* Is Gutierrez there? Secretary of State's Office.
ROSAMARIA: Just a minute. *(To Pepe:)* Secretary of State's Office.

Pepe makes a surprised gesture. Rosamaria gives him the phone.

ROSAMARIA: That's what he said.

Pepe takes the phone. Almost simultaneously, Efren gets up from his desk and goes to another phone, most certainly an extension. From there, hunched over, he listens to Pepe's phone conversation. While Pepe talks, Juan Jose looks over the document; Rosamaria watches him.

PEPE: *(Into the phone)* Gutierrez.
MOCTEZUMA PEON: This is Moctezuma Peon, Mr. Gutierrez. I'm not gonna mince words. I need those papers immediately. . . I'll be waiting for you in fifteen minutes, in front of Las Gondolas, on Puente de Alvarado. . . Your dear friend is about to have an accident.
PEPE: And the money?

Pepe's exclamation alerts Juan Jose and Rosamaria.

MOCTEZUMA PEON: I'll be waiting for you in fifteen minutes.

Moctezuma Peon hangs up the phone and disappears down the street. Assistants A and B are following him, very secretively, keeping a good distance.

Pepe hangs up the phone. Efren also hangs up the extension.

JUAN JOSE: What's up?
PEPE: Give me that.

Pepe jerks from Juan Jose the folder with the papers and makes a move to leave.

JUAN JOSE: Where are you going?

Pepe walks toward the exit of the News room. Juan Jose catches up with him at the exit.

JUAN JOSE: *(Grabbing Pepe, pulling at him)* Are you gonna sell them?
PEPE: Let go of me.
JUAN JOSE: Those papers aren't for business deals, Pepe, they're to raise hell with.
PEPE: I said let me go. . .
JUAN JOSE: We could get the Chamber of Deputies. . .
PEPE: Cut the honest guy crap.
JUAN JOSE: Sometimes you've gotta be honest.
PEPE: *(Breaking away, sarcastic)* Honest, you? I've seen you putting the moves on Rosamaria.

With this phrase, Pepe breaks away from Juan Jose with a final pull. The latter tries to grab him again, but Pepe knees him in the testicles and Juan Jose doubles over. Pepe leaves the News room running. The Shoeshine Boy puts the shoes aside and follows Pepe.

Efren dials a number.

Simultaneous Scenes

Space 3: In the Cantina, the phone rings. A few minutes earlier, while the Bartender was setting up, a loud knock on the metallic curtain was heard. The Bartender opened it and Agent 2 entered. Before Agent 2 can say anything to the Bartender, the phone rings. Agent 2 answers it.

Since Agent 2 hunches over the phone to speak, in the same position as Efren, we can't hear the brief conversation between the Cantina and the News room, just a few of Efren's words.

EFREN: I've got it. But I need. . .

Juan Jose is in pain from the blow to his testicles. Rosamaria helps him, disconcerted by what she has just heard Pepe say. Little by little, Juan Jose recovers.

JUAN JOSE: They're going to kill him.
ROSAMARIA: *(Thinking about the other)* He already knew. He found out.
JUAN JOSE: It's your fault. You're the whore.

Rosamaria is surprised by the insult. She gets angry. She is about to cry.

JUAN JOSE: If I don't catch him they'll kill him. *(He starts to leave.)* They're gonna kill him, Rosamaria.

Efren hangs up the phone and casually heads toward the door. As he leaves he crosses in front of Juan Jose and Rosamaria.

EFREN: *(Sarcastically)* I told you so, kids, I told you so...

Efren leaves. Juan Jose looks at Rosamaria for a few seconds and then leaves the building also. Rosamaria slowly returns to her desk, pensive, lost in thought. The Errand Boy looks at her with compassion.

Sagrario and Low Official emerge from the Editor's private office, almost at the same instant that Ric enters the News room, coming from a different area of the building. Editor Sagrario and Low Official head toward the door.

SAGRARIO: *(To Rosamaria)* If anything urgent comes up, I'm at Cantu's office. *(To Ric:)* Would you mind coming with us, Ricardo?

Editor Sagrario leaves, followed by Low Official and Ric.

SCENE 13

Week 2. Tuesday night and early Wednesday. Between 11:45 and 12:30 p.m.

Main action: Space 9: Cabaret

Simultaneous actions

Space 1:   News room

The News room is almost empty. Camarena the Mechanic explains to Rosamaria the hopeless situation with the photocopy machine and then he leaves. Rosamaria returns to her desk, holding back tears. The Errand Boy approaches, comforting.

Space 2:   Apartment Building

When Moctezuma Peon's Assistant finishes raping Dalila, he busies himself by snooping around the apartment and robbing small valuable items. He makes several telephone calls, but he is never able to get through. Dalila remains lifeless, stretched out on the sofa where she endured the attack.

Space 3:   Cantina

The Bartender pulls down the metal curtain again and prepares himself a drink.

Space 6:   Government Offices

High Official turns the television off. She starts looking over papers and making telephone calls. She seems nervous. At the end of the scene Low Official, Editor Sagrario and Ric arrive at the building of the Government Offices.

Space 7:   Taco Restaurant

Agent 2 arrives at the Taco Restaurant. He orders some tacos, which the Taco Seller prepares. He is waiting for Efren.

Space 8:   Gerda's Apartment

> *Never taking her eyes from the television, Gerda cleans the wounds of Pato the Masseur. She helps him stretch out on the sofa to rest; she gives him some tea to drink.*

Space 9: Cabaret

The Cabaret Las Gondolas is a second class club. On the overcrowded dance floor Assistants A and B dance with the call girls. The Florist is perhaps one of them. Assistants A and B seem to be discreetly watching Moctezuma Peon, who is at a corner table. He has in front of him a bottle of whiskey, a bucket of ice, mineral water and some glasses. He mixes himself a highball, which he then tastes.

Toño is at another table, drunk. He stands up and shouts when he sees Pepe arrives and recognizes him. Pepe comes in looking for someone at the tables.

TOÑO: Look who's here! The best journalist in Mexico! Pepe! Pepe! Come over here and sit with me. . . I need some advice, Pepe. They've fucked me over at the *Sol de Mexico*. They've taken away my beat, I'm out in the cold again. . . You've got to help me. I want to work with you, for your paper. You work for a real paper, Pepe.

Pepe barely manages to break free of Toño; the Waiter helps him push the drunken Toño away. Toño grabs the Waiter, shakes him and heads for the dance floor. He tries to dance with one of the call girls, but he collapses and falls to the floor at the edge of the dance floor. He remains there during the entire scene. The couples dance, almost stepping on him. No one is concerned about him.

Pepe finds Moctezuma Peon and goes to his table. The policeman offers him a seat.

MOCTEZUMA PEON: A highball, Mr. Gutierrez?

The loudness of the music makes it difficult to hear.

PEPE: I beg your pardon?

Moctezuma Peon makes himself understood by gesturing. Pepe nods and Moctezuma Peon mixes him a highball. They drink.

Space 1: News room

The Errand Boy approaches Rosamaria, who is very upset.

ROSAMARIA: They're gonna kill him, didn't you hear?
ERRAND BOY: I don't know anything about it.
ROSAMARIA: Don't play dumb... You heard Juan Jose. They're going to kill him.
ERRAND BOY: Who?
ROSAMARIA: Who do you think? Pepe.

The Errand Boy makes a sympathetic gesture and then returns to his work: he is looking for some photographs.

The music stops for a moment. There is a break.

MOCTEZUMA PEON: The papers?
PEPE: Where's Dalila?
MOCTEZUMA PEON: Is that the name of that crazy woman? Salcido's sister, right? Poor guy, he died prematurely.
PEPE: Where is she?
MOCTEZUMA PEON: Don't worry. You keep your end of the bargain, I'll keep mine.

Pause.

PEPE: You had mentioned some money.
MOCTEZUMA PEON: *(Smiling)* "had mentioned." You said it. That offer was like a store bargain: for a limited time only. It's over. Now the only dough I'm gonna come up with is the piece of tail... If you want it.
PEPE: What's going to happen to her?
MOCTEZUMA PEON: I don't know. Maybe a suicide in the subway... women nowadays frequently commit suicide. Or she could fall from a roof. I don't know.
PEPE: I want to see her first.
MOCTEZUMA PEON: No, my friend. I'm the one who sets the conditions. First, you hand those papers over to me and then I'll tell you where you can find the little piece.

PEPE: And if you're tricking me?
MOCTEZUMA PEON: Moctezuma Peon never tricks anyone.

Pepe becomes pensive. The loud music starts up again. The couples get up to dance. Pepe takes a long drink of his whiskey.

Space 7: Taco Restaurant
Efren arrives and meets up with Agent 2, who has finished his tacos. Efren looks at him. Agent 2 pulls out a bundle of bills and gives it to Efren. Efren looks at the bundle.   **EFREN:** We agreed you'd pay in dollars.   **AGENT:** I didn't get to the exchange on time.   *Efren starts counting the money. He finishes and makes a gesture of agreement to Agent 2. The latter leaves rapidly. Efren orders some tacos from the Taco Seller.*

Pepe finishes drinking his whiskey and then he takes the folder from the back of his suit coat and hands it to Moctezuma Peon. The latter takes it and finds a spot of light in which to examine it. He nods. He closes the folder. He says a few words to Pepe which are drowned out by the music. Pepe makes a gesture of displeasure and he gets up. He leaves the Cabaret.

When Moctezuma Peon is alone again at his table, Assistant A, who has been discreetly watching him from the dance floor, comes over to him. He greets Moctezuma Peon courteously and exchanges a few inaudible words with him. Moctezuma Peon asks Assistant A to sit down, but when the latter goes to do so, Moctezuma Peon turns the table over on top of him, knocking him ostentatiously to the ground. Moctezuma Peon takes off running toward the exit of the Cabaret. He knocks over some other tables as he goes. Assistant B, who was also watching Peon from the dance floor, runs after him and shoots, trying to cut him off. He is not successful. Moctezuma Peon disappears. Assistants A and B run after him. Shouting in the Cabaret. The Shoeshine Boy has been observing the scene and now also runs out of the Cabaret.

SCENE 14

Week 2. Early Wednesday. Between 0:30 and 1:15 a.m.

Main Action: Space 2: Apartment Building

Simultaneous actions
Space 1: News room
Only Rosamaria and the Errand Boy are in the News room. Rosamaria is at her desk, self-absorbed, crying quietly. The Errand Boy watches her from a distance.
Space 3: Cantina
After searching for Pepe with no luck, Juan Jose has ended up in the Cantina. The Bartender has let him in and closed up again. Juan Jose is drinking at the bar; he is already drunk.
Space 6: Government Offices
In the main office, High Official talks with Sagrario. Low Official office, in his office with Ric, appears to await orders.
Space 7: Taco Restaurant
Efren eats his tacos. The Taco Seller watches him.
Space 8: Gerda's House
Pato the Masseur has finally fallen asleep on the sofa, his head in Gerda's lap. The old woman caresses him as if he were her son, but she keeps her eyes on the television. She is also about to fall asleep.
Space 9: Cabaret

After Moctezuma Peon's flight, the waiters and call girls straighten up the place: they are picking up tables and chairs, sweeping up broken bottles. The music is playing again. Toño is still lying on the dance floor, drunk.

Space 2: Apartment Building

Dalila is still stretched out on the sofa, half naked and mentally absent. Moctezuma Peon's Assistant has finally managed to place his telephone call.

Simultaneous scenes

The phone rings in Space 9: Cabaret. Moctezuma Peon's Assistant calls from Dalila's Apartment. The Florist-Call girl answers.

FLORIST: Cabaret Las Gondolas.
PEON'S ASSISTANT: Is my boss there?
FLORIST: Who?
PEON'S ASSISTANT: My boss.
FLORIST: No, but your fairy godmother's here.
PEON'S ASSISTANT: Is this Tere?
FLORIST: Who's this?
PEON'S ASSISTANT: Is Mr. Moctezuma there?
FLORIST: He just left. He went out in a cloud of smoke. Gunfire.
PEON'S ASSISTANT: Gunfire?
FLORIST: Yeah, gunfire.

The Florist hangs up.

Moctezuma Peon's Assistant waits a moment before hanging up. He says into the phone:

PEON'S ASSISTANT: Oh, well, thank you very much. *(He hangs the phone up, doesn't move for a moment, while he thinks; then he leaves running.)*

A few seconds after Moctezuma Peon's Assistant leaves the building, Pepe arrives. He climbs the stairs hurriedly. The door to Apartment 5 is open. The room is dark.

PEPE: Dalila... Dalila, are you here?
DALILA: Pepe?

Pepe goes to the sofa. He realizes what has happened to Dalila.

PEPE: What did they do to you?
DALILA: I'm OK.
PEPE: What did they do to you, Dalila?
DALILA: It's over now. *(Silence.)* What about the papers? Are Chano's papers safe?
PEPE: Yes.
DALILA: Are they going to publish them in the newspaper?
PEPE: We're going to publish them.

Dalila seems to feel a little better. She sits up.

DALILA: In your paper?
PEPE: Not exactly... Tomorrow Juan Jose and I are going to take them to the opposition's deputies, so they can start bringing charges in Congress.
DALILA: That's what Chano wanted... A little justice, a little truth.
PEPE: Do you feel OK, Dalila?
DALILA: Wonderfully well.

Dalila seems to enter a trance. She recites:

DALILA:

> Pity me, I walk with a slow foot
> while time, fleeing, assures me
> of little count and a fatal moment.

Space 3: Cantina

Moctezuma Peon runs down the street fleeing from Assistants A and B. He bangs on the metal curtain. The Bartender and Juan Jose are inside.

MOCTEZUMA PEON: Open up, Blackie.

The Bartender opens and lets Moctezuma Peon enter. He closes up again. With a gesture, Moctezuma Peon asks for a place to hide. The Bartender hides him under the bar.

A few seconds later, Assistants A and B beat on the curtain.

ASST A: Police! Police!

The Bartender opens the metal curtain. Assistants A and B enter. They look for Moctezuma Peon but can't find him. They leave, running. As soon as they have gone, the Bartender informs Moctezuma Peon.

BARTENDER: They're gone, boss.

Moctezuma Peon leaves his hiding place and starts running down the street.

DALILA:

>It's sad, that autumn is coming on
>and I'm still the unplanted seed
>the tree whose fruit never ripened.

Space 1: News room
The Errand Boy comes to Rosamaria, who is still crying quietly at her desk.
ERRAND BOY: *(Affectionately)* Don't cry, Rosita. He's not the only man in the world.

DALILA:

>How is it that my soul is so calm
>when it sees its treasure
>turned into a confusing breath of nothingness?

> **Space 7: Taco Restaurant**
>
> *With his plate of tacos in front of him, Efren takes from his pocket, for the nth time, the bundle of bills given to him by Agent 2. He counts them. The Taco Seller comes forward:*
>
> **TACO SELLER:** *(Maliciously)* Aren't you going to share, boss?

DALILA:

> What is it, under the dust, that I so adore, though vile
> This ephemeral gift which is devoured
> When I enjoy it?
>
> Like a dart that hits its target expertly
> Like the stone broken away from the center,
> So goes my body to its final destiny.

> **Space 3: Cantina**
>
> *Now Moctezuma Peon's Assistant is beating on the closed metal curtain. The Bartender opens it.*
>
> **PEON'S ASSISTANT:** Have you seen my boss?
> **BARTENDER:** He just left. Some thugs are after him . . . they're armed.
>
> *Moctezuma Peon's Assistant leaves, running. Disconnected from the scene, Juan Jose is very drunk now. He has left the bar and taken a seat at one of the tables. He drinks.*
>
> **JUAN JOSE:** Stinkin' Pepe. . . We would have caused the biggest scandal ever, stinkin' Pepe.

DALILA:

> The sad good-bye will take place there
> Between these two, who have loved without measure
> There my soul with wounded pain,

> When on its dark grave
> It abandons this body against its will
> The body it loved so fearlessly and foolishly.

Space 9: Cabaret

Things are back to normal. Everyone is dancing. Waitress Antonia has arrived and barely manages to rescue Toño from the dance floor, where he is lying. She pulls him on to her lap, caresses him maternally.

TOÑO: Don't leave me, Antonia, don't leave me.

DALILA:

> Will you then take in the Loved One,
> Who waited in vain while he lived
> And was cruelly passed over?

Space 4: The Street

Moctezuma Peon, fleeing down a narrow, dark, empty street, runs into Agent 2. The latter blocks his escape and tries to be conciliatory. He is about to speak when Assistants A and B emerge from the darkness. Assistant A points a pistol at him.
ASST A: Quiet, Moctezuma.

Agent 2 steps back so as not to be seen. Asst. A moves forward. Moctezuma shoots him with a rapid movement. Assistant A seems to be wounded and when Moctezuma Peon is going to take off running again, Assistant B blocks his path.

ASSISTANT B: The papers.

Moctezuma Peon tries to flee, but Assistant B pushes him. Assistant B and Assistant A, who has recovered, beat him violently. Assistant B finally strangles him with a wire. During the scuffle, the folder has fallen to the ground. Agent 2 comes out of the shadows and tries to pick it up, but Assistant A shoots him repeatedly. The bodies of Moctezuma Peon and Agent 2 remain stretched out in the narrow street. Assistants A and B get into a car and disappear, having recovered the folder.

Minutes later Moctezuma Peon's Assistant reaches the narrow street and finds his boss' body. He grabs his legs, embraces him, whines.

PEON'S ASSISTANT: Boss... boss...

DALILA:

> No, it's true that on the evening of his day,
> Knowing himself to be guilty, evil and low
> He would not dare to remember even God,
>
> Preferring the fiery whirlwind,
> Eternal darkness, everlasting flames
> To the reproaches of love divine.
>
> Look, then, and know what you love,
> Oh, poor blind and wandering desire
> You who throw yourself into the arms of deceit.

Dalila embraces Pepe. She will remain in this embrace until the end of the scene.

Space 6:   Government Offices

Assistants A and B arrive at High Official's Office with the folder. They give it to her. Sagrario, Low Official, Ric and the Shoeshine Boy witness the scene. Low Official is on the network phone and passes the receiver to High Official.

HIGH OFFICIAL: *(Into the phone)* We got it, sir. *(She smiles happily and says to the Editor, while she hands her the receiver:)* He would like to speak to you.

Editor Sagrario takes the phone.

SAGRARIO: *(Into the phone)*
--Yes, sir.

--Yes, sir.

--Yes, sir.

Sagrario returns the receiver to High Official.

HIGH OFFICIAL: *(Into the phone)* That's what we're here for, Mr. President.

Space 8: Gerda's House

Gerda and Pato the Masseur have fallen asleep in front of the television set. The last program of the day is finishing. On the screen: the image of a group of cadets lowering the flag. A chorus sings the National Anthem.

FINAL DARKNESS